THE
RAW FOOD
HEALING BIBLE

METRO BOOKS
New York

An Imprint of Sterling Publishing
1166 Avenue of the Americas
New York, NY 10036

METRO BOOKS and the distinctive Metro Books logo are trademarks of Sterling Publishing Co., Inc.

This book was designed, conceived, and produced by
Quantum Books Ltd
6 Blundell Street
London N7 9BH
United Kingdom

Publisher: Kerry Enzor
Design: Paul Turner and Sue Pressley,
Stonecastle Graphics
Copyeditors: Kathy Steer and Philip de Ste. Croix
Senior Editor: Philippa Davis
Publishing Assistant: Emma Harverson
Production Manager: Zarni Win
Cover Design: Tokiko Morishima

ISBN 978-1-4351-6117-7 (print format)

For information about custom editions, special sales, and premium and corporate purchases, please contact Sterling Special Sales at 800-805-5489 or specialsales@sterlingpublishing.com.

Printed in China by 1010 Printing International Ltd

2 4 6 8 10 9 7 5 3 1

www.sterlingpublishing.com

THE
RAW FOOD
HEALING BIBLE

Christine Bailey

METRO BOOKS
New York

Contents

Disclaimer

This book is intended for general informational purposes only and should not be relied upon as recommending or promoting any specific practice or method of treatment. It is not intended to diagnose, treat, or prevent any illness or condition and is not a substitute for advice from a health care professional.

You should consult your medical practitioner before starting any diet, fast, exercise, or supplementation program, and before taking any medication or nutritional supplement. You should not use the information in this book as a substitute for medication or other treatment prescribed by your medical practitioner.

There is the possibility of allergic or other adverse reactions from the use of any product mentioned in this book. In particular, those with medical conditions or allergies, the young, the old, and pregnant women should seek further advice from their medical practitioner before taking any medication or nutritional supplement or making changes to their diet.

The publisher and the author make no representations or warranties with respect to the accuracy, completeness, or currency of the contents of this work, and specifically disclaim, without limitation, any implied warranties of merchantability or fitness for a particular purpose and any injury, illness, damage, liability, or loss incurred, directly or indirectly, from the use or application of any of the contents of this book.

The publisher and the author are not affiliated with and do not sponsor or endorse any websites, organizations, or other sources of information referred to herein, and the publisher and the author do not warrant the accuracy, completeness, or currency of any information or recommendations provided by those sources.

All trademarks, service marks, and trade names used herein are the property of their respective owners and are used only to identify the products or services of those owners. The publisher and the author are not associated with any product, service, or vendor mentioned in this book and this book is not licensed or endorsed by the owner of any trademark, service mark or trade name appearing herein. The publisher and the author do not recommend, endorse, or encourage the use of any product mentioned in this book, make any representations or warranties as to any product mentioned herein, or warrant the accuracy of any claims which the manufacturer or distributor of any product may make with respect to that product.

Introduction

The raw food diet has been rapidly gaining popularity over the past ten to 15 years with raw food magazines, books, blogs, websites, and restaurants now commonplace. Whether you are looking to follow a largely raw food diet or simply wish to increase your intake of raw foods, you will find *The Raw Food Healing Bible* an essential resource. If you find the thought of eating just raw foods daunting this book will provide you with lots of practical tips, nutritional advice, and recipes to inspire and motivate you.

Raw food is more than just a diet. For many it is an entire philosophy and way of life. Eating more fresh, organic ingredients affects the way we look and feel and how we interact with our environment. Many people following a raw food diet also adopt a more toxic-free lifestyle—this may include choosing chemical-free cleaning products, organic cosmetics and personal products, filtered water systems, and being conscious of living lightly on the earth—recycling and enjoying local seasonal produce.

About the Author

Christine Bailey is an award winning nutritional therapist, chef, author, and broadcaster with over 18 years of experience in the health industry. With a passion for creating delicious nourishing recipes, Christine has a reputation for transforming people's health and inspiring love of real food. Working in the food, health, and fitness sector, Christine is much sought after due to her in-depth nutritional and food expertise.

Living Raw

What is the Raw Food Diet?

What is raw food? Simply put, raw food is uncooked food that has not been heated to above 118°F (47°C). It is typically pure, unadulterated, whole food, which is rich in vitamins, minerals, phytonutrients, and enzymes. The term "living foods" generally refers to foods that are still alive and growing, i.e. they are uncooked and unheated, like sprouted beans, pulses or legumes (see page 28), seeds, and living greens, such as wheatgrass and sunflower greens.

A raw food diet is one based around plenty of vegetables, especially green leafy vegetables, fruit, nuts, sprouted grains, beans or pulses, and seeds. It does not include any processed or refined foods. Liquids are also an essential part of the diet in the form of pure filtered water, fresh juices, herbal infusions, nut or seed milks, and smoothies.

Both living foods and raw foods contain a wide range of vitamins, minerals, enzymes, and phytonutrients that are essential for the proper maintenance of the body. However, the difference between living foods and raw food is that living foods contain a higher amount of health-promoting enzymes than raw food. In raw food the enzymes are dormant. To activate these enzymes the food, such as nuts, grains, or seeds need to be soaked first. This also makes them more digestible.

The use of dehydrators in a raw food diet can also add variety to fresh produce by creating dried dishes like granola, crackers, and Easy Kale Chips (see page 27).

Variations of the Raw Food Diet

Typically those following a raw food diet consume at least 70 percent or more of their food raw. Most raw foodists eat no animal products at all and follow a strict vegan diet. Some people, however, may include raw eggs, nonpasteurized milk products, and bee products (bee pollen, propolis, and honey) and follow a raw vegetarian diet.

With the popularity of the paleo diet some people are adopting a paleo-raw style of eating and include raw eggs, fish (sashimi), meat (carpaccio), and unpasteurized dairy products (see page 18).

Opposite: Most people who adopt a raw food lifestyle eat only a strict vegan diet based around plenty of vegetables, fruit, nuts, sprouted grains, beans, and seeds.

Why Choose the Raw Food Diet?

There are many reasons why people may choose to adopt a raw food diet. Often, it can be an extremely effective way to lose weight and/or maintain a healthy weight. However, there are many other potential benefits from eating more raw foods.

Packed with Nutrients

Raw foods, such as raw sprouted seeds and beans, vegetables, herbs, and fruits are incredibly nutrient dense and are packed with a wealth of fiber, vitamins, minerals, and phytonutrients, plant compounds known for their protective antioxidant properties.

Rich in Enzymes

Those following a raw food diet believe that raw foods contain essential food enzymes and nutrients that are destroyed or altered if the food is heated to above 118°F (47°C). Enzymes are required for numerous chemical and metabolic processes in our body, including energy production and detoxification. By incorporating more raw food into your diet, you are providing your body with an abundance of the essential enzymes, nutrients, and fiber that it needs to process food, detoxify, create energy, and perform at its optimum.

Support the Liver

When the liver is overworked and we can't detoxify effectively, waste products and toxins can be stored in our fat cells—the more toxins in our bodies, the more fat cells are needed, and the harder it can be to lose weight. An increase in toxins can also lead to inflammation, which can damage tissues and accelerate the signs of aging. Raw foods are rich in nutrients to help cleanse and detoxify the body. A raw food diet works in many ways: on the one hand you are providing your body with nutrients to help it function more effectively and clean itself, while also avoiding foods that diminish the efficiency of cleansing and detoxification.

Help to Boost Energy Levels

By nourishing your body with essential vitamins, minerals, supporting digestion and absorption of nutrients, and reducing toxic overload, you can help boost energy levels and improve mental clarity.

Stay Hydrated

Raw foods are hydrating and satiating as they are high in fiber. This enables you to feel fuller for longer while also keeping energy levels high.

Alkalize Your Body

Fruits and vegetables, especially raw leafy greens which are full of chlorophyll, have the added benefit of being incredibly alkalizing. Eating cooked, processed foods and animal products increases our body's acidity. Too many acid forming foods can lead to a lack of energy, promote inflammation, lower the immune system, increase weight, and reduce the levels of alkaline minerals, such as calcium and magnesium. By increasing your intake of alkalizing foods and drinks you help to restore your body's pH balance, enabling it to heal and regenerate more effectively.

Potential Health Benefits of a Raw Food Diet

Here are some of the potential benefits people experience following a raw food based diet:

- Lose weight
- Improve digestion
- Increase energy and vitality
- Improve immune system—fewer colds and infections
- Have a clearer, more radiant complexion and healthier hair
- Improve mental clarity
- Relief from allergies
- Reduce the risk of heart disease, diabetes, and other serious chronic conditions.

The Raw Food Pantry

If you're looking to adopt a raw food diet the list below will guide you. Not all of the ingredients are 100 percent raw, such as xylitol, stevia, or tamari, but these are healthy, nutritious additions to enhance the flavor and texture of raw food dishes and are generally accepted as being included in a raw food diet.

What's Included in the Raw Food Diet?

- Fresh and frozen vegetables
- Sea vegetables: including kelp noodles, nori sheets, sea vegetable salad mix, and nori, kelp, and dulse flakes
- Supergreen powders: chlorella, Klamath lake blue green algae, and spirulina (avoid algae supplements if you suffer with an iodine allergy). Moringa leaf powder, green tea, and green tea matcha powder
- Supergrass powders: barley grass powder, wheatgrass powder, supergreens blend
- Sprouted seeds
- Superherbs: fresh herbs such as parsley, mint, cilantro, basil, sage, thyme, and ashwagandha; and powders, teas, tinctures, or juices including maca powder, ground turmeric, aloe vera juice, ginseng, he shou wu, shilajit

powder, gynostemma, mucuna pruriens, and schizandra
- Medicinal mushrooms: chaga, cordyceps, maitake, reishi, fresh, dried, powdered blends, and tinctures
- Ready sprouted seeds and beans or dry beans/seeds to sprout: alfalfa, broccoli sprouts, fenugreek sprouts, lentil sprouts, pea shoots, mung bean sprouts, sunflower seed sprouts, quinoa sprouts, buckwheat sprouts
- Fresh and frozen fruit
- Superfruits: acai berry, amla berry, incan, baobab, camu camu berry, goji berry, macqui berry, lucuma, mulberry, noni fruit. They are available as powder or as dried fruit
- Nuts and seeds: includes raw nuts and seeds (whole and ground), activated nuts (see page 28), seed and nut oils, nut and seed butters and spreads, tahini, buckwheat groats, quinoa, coconut flakes, dry unsweetened coconut
- Raw chocolate: cacao powder, butter, raw chocolates, cacao beans, and nibs
- Raw fermented foods: sauerkraut, kimchi, nut yogurt, coconut yogurt, water kefir, raw milk kefir, coconut kefir, raw pickles, kombucha, and rejuvelac
- Oils: coconut oil, omega blended oils, pumpkin seed oil, avocado oil, extra

virgin olive oil, flaxseed, hemp seed oil, sesame oil, macadamia nut oil, chia seed oil, and walnut oil

- Condiments: apple cider vinegar, rice, balsamic, and red wine vinegars, white miso paste, liquid aminos, or tamari, Nama Shoyu (raw soy sauce), marinated sundried tomatoes, mustard, olives
- Flavorings: sea salt, herbal salts, garlic salt, freshly ground black pepper, nutritional yeast flakes, tahini, vanilla extract, spices, and herbs
- Sweeteners: xylitol, erythritol, Lo Han Guo, coconut sugar, yacon syrup, palymra jaggery, maple syrup, stevia, lucuma, dried fruits, raw honey, bee and flower pollen
- Dehydrated products: raw granola, dried fruits and vegetables, kale chips, raw seeded crackers, raw pizza, coconut wraps, raw cookies and bars, activated and dried nuts, chewy fruit, and vegetable leathers
- Protein powders: vegan protein powders (hemp, rice, sprouted seeds, pea, spirulina)
- Bee products: flower and bee pollen, propolis, raw honey, royal jelly
- Raw meat, dairy, eggs, and fish (optional, not vegan).

Nutritional Considerations

Those following a raw food based diet will need to be mindful of keeping themselves optimally nourished. Including nutrient-dense superfoods in your diet can be helpful, but supplementation may also be required.

Protein—This can be in low supply on a raw food diet. Protein rich vegan foods include sprouted grains, beans, nuts and seeds and their butters, coconut kefir and yogurt, spirulina, leafy green vegetables, and mushrooms. A variety of sources will ensure that you get all the essential amino acids. Protein powders can also be helpful. These are often based around rice protein, hemp, pea, or sprouted beans and seeds and can be bought from health food stores. Add to smoothies.

Vitamin B12—It is difficult to obtain enough B12 on some raw vegan diets. While some foods may contain B12 it is not clear how absorbable these are and they should not be relied on as a B12 source. There are many vegan foods fortified with B12, such as some brands of nutritional yeast flakes and cereals, but they may not necessarily be suitable to eat raw. Supplementation is recommended and tablets are available in pharmacies and health food stores.

Vitamin D—Modern lifestyles make it difficult to get adequate vitamin D from sunshine based synthesis and a vegan raw food based diet is also more likely to be deficient. A daily supplement, especially during the winter months, may be beneficial. You can buy vitamin D tablets in pharmacies and health food stores.

Iron—Good vegan raw sources of iron include leafy green vegetables, sprouted lentils and beans, cashew nuts, sesame, raw chocolate, pumpkin seeds, and dried apricots. Women may need to eat a little more iron-rich foods especially if pregnant.

Essential omega-3 fat—To optimize essential fats in the body include omega-3 rich foods daily, such as chia, flaxseed, walnut, hemp, and leafy greens. As conversion to the active omega-3 fats are limited in a raw food diet, a vegan supplement may be recommended. Buy vegan algae oil blends, capsules, or tablets from pharmacies and health food stores.

Choline—This is important for certain brain functions and lipid metabolism; it can be found in quinoa and lecithin powders (derived from soy and sunflower). Buy from health food stores and use in smoothies.

Creating a Healthy Raw Food Diet

For a healthy balanced raw food diet it is important to eat enough protein, healthy fats, and slow releasing carbohydrates. Every day, focus on eating plenty of organic vegetables including lots of leafy greens. Make sure there is a selection of colorful vegetables in each meal you prepare, together with a variety of healthy fats and protein rich foods.

Avoid the temptation to overdose on fruits, particularly dried fruit, as it can disrupt blood sugar balance. Preparation and organization are the key to achieving a healthy balanced diet. Make sure that you have soaked nuts and seeds, and also prepared raw crackers, sprouts, and fermented foods and drinks—this will make daily life a lot easier for you.

Raw Meat, Fish, Dairy, and Eggs

Some people adopting a raw food diet also include raw meat, fish (as shown below), dairy, and eggs. If you are considering including such foods you must think about safety. Quality is of paramount importance—only select foods from trusted quality suppliers, grass fed, organic, and very fresh. Some people freeze the meat for 14 days before consuming, which helps to kill potentially harmful pathogens. You may also wish to marinate meat and fish prior to eating—for example, ceviche is a popular raw marinated fish dish. Food-borne illness is a serious concern and for this reason it is extremely important to follow good food hygiene practices— storing foods at the right temperature, washing your hands, and sanitizing counters and cutting boards.

Raw milk has not been pasteurized or heat treated to kill any bacteria present. In some US states, raw milk sales are banned because it can carry harmful bacteria that may pose a health risk. In many European

countries it is possible to buy raw milk from farms. Disease-causing bacteria can enter the milk through bad hygiene practices and during milking, so the quality of the milk and cleanliness is very important. Many people prefer to drink raw milk as it is richer in enzymes, beneficial bacteria, and has a higher vitamin content. For some, it is also easier to digest.

Eggs (as shown above) are rich in protein, fat, vitamins, minerals, and antioxidants; raw eggs have a greater nutritional profile than cooked eggs and many people find them easier to digest. Antioxidant levels—lutein and zeaxanthin, a class of carotenoids present in eggs—are much higher in raw eggs than in cooked ones. Raw eggs can be added to smoothies. As with meat and fish quality is important. Choose eggs from pastured organic hens. The salmonella risk is increased when hens are raised in unsanitary conditions, which is less likely on organic farms where the chickens are raised in clean, spacious conditions, and forage around for food.

There have been concerns that overconsuming egg whites can lead to biotin deficiency. This is because egg whites contain a glycoprotein called avidin that is effective at binding biotin, one of the B vitamins. For this reason, some people prefer to only eat raw egg yolks. However, as egg yolks are rich in biotin it is unlikely that eating the whole egg raw will lead to a biotin deficiency.

The Raw Food Kitchen

A raw food diet does not have to mean expensive equipment and gadgets. You can start with just a few basic items and gradually build up according to the type of recipes you like to eat. The most useful pieces of equipment are probably a high speed blender and food processor. Here are some popular pieces of equipment and gadgets that may be helpful.

High Speed Blender

A high speed blender is powerful enough to grind up nuts, seeds, and ice as well as creating raw soups, nut butters, smoothies, nut and seed milks, desserts, and delicious raw sauces.

Single-Serve Blenders

Brands such as the Nutribullet extractor and Tribest's blender (see below left) are ideal for making single-serve smoothies. They come with several blades to enable you to make smoothies and grind nuts, seeds, and spices.

Food Processor

A good food processor (see opposite) is the perfect tool for blending ingredients as well as chopping, slicing, and grating easily, so is ideal when preparing vegetables. If you can afford it choose a robust, durable model with a good range of grating and slicing options. A blender, on the other hand, blends mixtures into a smooth uniform texture so is great for raw soups, smoothies, and salad dressings. Food processors can also pulverize nuts and seeds for using to make nut milk and cheese.

Juicer

If you are keen on making green juices then choose a masticating juicer, as this will enable you to extract the greatest amount of nutrients from your fruit and vegetables including leafy greens. Masticating juicers "chew," or masticate your produce by grinding (like teeth) and then squeezing the juice out.

Nut Milk Bag

Nut milk bags are lightweight, sturdy cheesecloth bags used for making nut milks. They can be used over and over again and usually have a drawstring to help you get all the liquid out of the pulp.

Dehydrator

A dehydrator (see below) is used to dry foods at low temperatures (below 118°F/48°C) while preserving the nutrient content and enzymes of the food. These are expensive but worth the investment if you are planning to follow a raw food diet. They are perfect for creating "cooked"-like dishes, warming foods, or making crackers, chips, breads, and wraps. Use them to make your own dried fruit, fruit leathers, and vegetable chips (see page 27) for delicious healthy snacks. While many modern ovens are able to cook at low temperatures (104–113°F/40–45°C) they will not create the same texture as a dehydrator. If you are making raw crackers, breads, or fruit leather then the shelves need to be lined with special nonstick lining sheets. When choosing a dehydrator choose a model with a built-in timer.

Spiralizer

Spiralizers (see below) are ideal for making vegetable noodles like zucchini or carrot noodles, which can be tossed in a raw sauce or dressing. There are numerous models available, ranging from expensive, heavy-duty stand spiralizers to cheaper

handheld ones. The handheld spiralizer is extremely easy to use and is very similar to a pencil sharpener while other models are attached to the counter and the vegetables are pushed through with a turn of a handle. Most spiralizers come with at least two different blades to create ribbons and spiral shapes. Alternatively, use a vegetable peeler or the grating attachment on your food processor.

Mandolin Slicer

A mandolin (as shown above) helps slice vegetables thinly giving you consistent slices—these can be useful for creating vegetable and fruit chips in a dehydrator.

Mason Jars

These glass jars with tight-fitting lids are very useful when making fermented vegetables and fermented drinks as well as storing raw soups, smoothies, juices, granola, and salads. Purchase a selection of sizes—1 quart and 1 pint jars are useful.

Sprouter

There are a range of sprouters available that can be useful to create your own selection of sprouted beans, seeds, and grains. Alternatively, you can simply use glass jars covered with cheesecloth or a mesh lid. Just make sure the jars are clean and sterilized before using.

Raw Food Techniques

Juicing

Preparing fresh juices is very popular on a raw food diet. Fruit juices are not recommended due to their high sugar and fructose content, which will upset blood sugar balance and lead to energy fluctuations and weight gain. To minimize sugar content focus on green based juices instead. These are prepared using around 80 percent vegetables with 20 percent fruit. Typically, apples, pears, and citrus fruits are popular choices but any fruit can be used. Citrus fruits are particularly low in fructose and can cut through the bitter taste of leafy vegetables. Green juices are packed with essential nutrients that are easily assimilated by the body. Drinking a green juice first thing in the morning is one of the best ways to give yourself a natural energy boost without resorting to stimulants like coffee.

There are lots of reasons why you should incorporate green juices into your daily diet. Firstly, juicing helps you to absorb all the nutrients from the vegetables. Many of us have compromised digestion—whether that's due to poor diet, stress, or lifestyle habits—so juicing will help to "predigest" nutrients allowing us to absorb and utilize them more efficiently. They are also extremely alkaline so are good for balancing acidity in the body. Green juices also enable us to consume a healthier amount of vegetables easily—you can cram in a whole array of nutrient packed greens in one glassful. Green juicing is also a great way to experiment with new vegetables, increasing the variety in your diet, which in turn can then increase your intake of vital nutrients.

Juices or Smoothies?

Juices don't contain the insoluble fiber from the fruit or vegetables used so the nutrients are highly concentrated and are quickly absorbed by the body. Smoothies retain all the fiber and this slows down digestion, making you feel fuller for longer. As smoothies are simply blended vegetables and fruit they are generally much faster to prepare than juices.

Opposite: Using a masticating juicer you can make a wide range of delicious healthy drinks from a variety of fresh fruit and vegetables. Combine citrus fruits with leafy green vegetables to make the juice sweeter.

Dehydrating

Although a dehydrator (see below) is not strictly necessary for a raw food diet it is a great way to increase the variety of foods eaten. It will enable you to make raw crackers, breads, pizza crusts, pie cases, kale chips (see opposite), dehydrated fruit and vegetable chips, granolas, and fruit leathers. It is important to properly dehydrate foods like crackers and breads

otherwise they may go moldy quickly. Many recipes require dehydrating for several hours or even overnight, so you may wish to double or triple the recipes and fill the dehydrator. This will ensure that you have plenty of prepared foods to hand. If you don't have a dehydrator, preheat your oven to its lowest setting and dry the food in the oven with the oven door propped open to avoid it overheating.

Easy Kale Chips

HEART HEALTH

Kale chips are simple to prepare and are perfect for a snack. If you don't have a dehydrator, then preheat your oven to its lowest setting, spread the coated kale on baking sheets, and dry in the oven, turning them every 20 minutes for about an hour until crisp.

Prep: 15 mins/Dry: 4 to 6 hrs

Ingredients (serves 4)

2 bunches of kale
3 tablespoons olive oil
1 tablespoon lemon juice
2 tablespoons nutritional yeast flakes
½ teaspoon sea salt

Method

1 Wash the kale and dry well. Remove and discard the tough stems and coarsely chop the leaves into bite-size pieces.

2 Put the olive oil, lemon juice, nutritional yeast flakes, and sea salt in a large bowl and stir well until combined. Add the kale and, using your hands, massage the oil into the leaves until the kale is coated all over.

3 Arrange the kale on nonstick sheets and dehydrate at 115°F (45°C) for 4 to 6 hours or until crisp.

EXCELLENT FOR KEEPING BONES STRONG	
Calories (per serving)	135
Protein	3.7 g
Total fat	10.8 g
of which saturated fat	1.4 g
Carbohydrates	8.9 g
of which sugars	1.4 g
Vitamins/minerals	A, C, calcium, copper

Soaking and Sprouting

Soaking nuts and seeds before using improves their digestibility by helping to reduce the plant's enzyme inhibitors (a molecule that interacts with an enzyme and stops it from working in its normal way) and also makes them easier to blend when making smoothies, nut milks, etc. However, if you are short of time you can use them without soaking first. Generally it is recommended to soak nuts for at least two hours before rinsing and using. It is also possible to sprout nuts and seeds but first make sure they are truly raw and have not been processed or heat treated.

Beans, pulses, legumes, grains, and certain seeds require soaking and sprouting before they can be eaten raw.

An exception are kidney beans, which should never be eaten raw as they contain a dangerous toxin.

Sprouting is essentially germinating the plant to create a "living food." This leads to a rapid increase in the vitamin content as well as making the protein, fats, and carbohydrates in the food much easier to digest and assimilate.

Before sprouting you need to soak the dry seed or bean in clean filtered water. While the soaking time varies (see chart, opposite) the easiest way is to soak them

Below: Nuts, seeds, grains, and beans are full of nutrients and are easy to soak and sprout, making them tasty and digestible.

Bean/seed	Soaking time	Sprouting time
Aduki	Overnight	5 to 6 days
Alfalfa	4 to 6 hours	5 days
Almonds	8 to 10 hours	1 to 2 days
Broccoli	4 to 8 hours	3 to 4 days
Buckwheat	Overnight	2 to 3 days
Chickpeas	Overnight	3 to 4 days
Fenugreek	4 to 8 hours	3 to 5 days
Kale	4 to 5 hours	5 days
Lentils	4 to 8 hours	3 to 4 days
Millet	Overnight	2 to 3 days
Mung bean	Overnight	5 days
Mustard	5 hours	5 days
Oat groats	6 to 8 hours	2 to 3 days
Pumpkin seeds	8 hours or overnight	1 day
Quinoa	2 to 3 hours	1 to 2 days
Radish	Overnight	5 days
Sunflower	4 to 5 hours	2 days
Wild rice	Overnight (at least 9 hours)	3 to 5 days

overnight, then rinse and drain thoroughly in the morning. Place the seeds or beans in a sprouter or clean jar, cover with a piece of cheesecloth or a mesh lid, then rinse and drain daily until they are ready to use (see chart above for sprouting times). It is important to drain the sprouts thoroughly after soaking and rinsing to reduce the risk of mold forming.

The quantity of sprouts produced from dry seed varies but as a general rule one cup of dry seeds or beans will yield around two to three cups of sprouts.

Grains, such as quinoa and wild rice, can also be sprouted. A few seeds, such as wheatgrass, sunflower greens, pea greens, and buckwheat greens, require planting in shallow soil after soaking.

Fermenting and Pickling

Pickling is not necessarily the same as fermenting foods. Pickling is an easy way to preserve food, especially if you have a glut of homegrown produce during the warmer months, and creates a tangy slightly sour taste, which can add extra flavor to dishes. Pickling is often done using vinegar whereas fermenting uses a starter, salt, and water to create its own acidic liquid to preserve food. There is no heat or pressure involved in fermentation, as good bacteria do the work.

Fermented foods are beneficial as they provide a good source of probiotic bacteria. These foods are usually prepared with a salt water or brine solution that allows natural bacteria to flourish during the fermentation process. Examples of popular fermented foods include sauerkraut (see below) and kimchi, which generally uses cabbage as the main ingredient. Fermented foods are highly recommended as a regular part of any diet to help support the digestive and immune systems. As they are "predigested" (the bacteria has broken down the naturally occurring sugars in the food so you don't have to), fermented foods are often easier to digest and some of the nutrients are more bioavailable. Fermented drinks, such as kombucha and rejuvelac, are also helpful in improving digestion and providing healthy bacteria for the gut.

Making the Transition to a Raw Food Diet

For those looking to increase their intake of raw food it is best to start slowly. This may include starting the day with a green juice or smoothie (see below) instead of your traditional breakfast, or switching to a raw salad for lunch or dinner. Begin by having two raw meals a day and keep one cooked meal, then increase the amount of raw food you have in your diet and gradually replace the cooked food with a raw meal. Having a range of prepared raw foods and snacks to hand can be very helpful if you are rushed for time. Start experimenting with different food preparation techniques to add more variety, for example, sprouting seeds and beans, and spiralizing zucchini and carrots are simple ways to increase your intake of raw foods.

Transitioning to a fully raw food diet can take time, but go at a pace that's comfortable and feels normal and natural for you.

You will also find a range of delicious raw food recipes in this book to get you started on your new diet.

Meal Planning

Before you start on your raw food journey it's worth stocking up on key pantry items to help you create delicious recipes and meals. Ideally, choose fresh local produce and adapt recipes according to vegetables and fruits in season. Some of the main pantry items that you will need are highlighted on pages 172–185. They include nuts, seeds, nut and seed butters, dried fruits, oils (coconut oil, olive, avocado, etc.), dried sea vegetables, sweeteners (e.g. stevia, yacon, xylitol, honey), dried herbs, spices, vanilla, condiments (apple cider vinegar, liquid aminos, and miso), and dried beans and seeds for sprouting.

What Do I Eat?

Following a raw food diet may feel daunting to start, so here are some suggestions to help you get started.

Breakfast

Green juices and smoothies are simple options for breakfast. Include some protein and healthy fat to help stabilize blood sugar levels and boost your energy. Other alternatives are fruit with nut yogurts, raw granola, soaked muesli, buckwheat cereals, and coconut kefir. You can also make raw crackers and breads and serve with nut butters or dips or make raw pancakes and crepes. For a savory option try sliced avocado with a selection of vegetables, or a salsa, olives, nuts, and seeds. Nut spreads are also delicious served with crackers.

Lunch and Dinner

Lunch and dinner options are interchangeable depending on preferences. A colorful salad with some additional protein (nut cheese, sprouted beans and seeds) is light and energizing. If you need a little starch add raw crackers or breads. Raw soups are delicious and take minutes to prepare with a high speed blender. If it's cold you can warm soups in a dehydrator before serving. Zucchini, carrot, or kelp noodles, raw coconut wraps, or nori wraps are other easy options. If you have a dehydrator marinate portobello mushrooms in a mixture of Nama Shoyu and olive oil then dehydrate for two hours and eat with a salad.

Raw Food Snacks

If you find that you need a snack in between meals it is best to keep it simple. This could include a handful of nuts and seeds, some fruits, vegetable sticks with nut butter, nut cheese, or a smoothie. Raw crackers, granola, nut yogurt, or fermented foods like sauerkraut are also good options.

Example Meal Planner

Remember to consume plenty of fluids each day—including water, green tea, herbal teas, coconut water, nut milks, green smoothies, kefir, and kombucha.

Breakfast	Lunch	Dinner	Snacks
Tropical Green Smoothie (p.120)	Kale Salad with Pumpkin Seeds and Cranberries (p.46); Raw Chocolate Cookie (p.146)	Vegan Tart with Creamy Cheese Filling (p.184); Mixed salad	Sauerkraut; Green Appleade (p.131)
Coconut Berry Chia Pudding (p.170)	Spiralized zucchini and carrot noodles; Pistachio Pesto (p.90); Raw crackers	Nori Rolls with Sushi Rice and Sweet Dipping Sauce (p.78); Supergreen Mint and Cacao Ice Cream (p.86)	Nut milk or coconut kefir; Honey Pistachio Halva (p.182)
Orange Mango Nut Yogurt (p.116); Green juice	Mixed salad with Asian Dressing (p.166) and nut cheese; Raw Fig Bars (p.126)	Citrus Chili Guacamole (p.57); Raw crackers; Mixed salad	Kombucha (p.158); Raw Fig Bars (p.126)
Chocolate Almond Nut Milk (p.195); Raw coconut bacon with marinated mushrooms, olives and tomatoes	Lettuce, Cucumber, and Mint Soup (p.53); Raw crackers	Mushroom Meatballs (p.101) with salad and kelp or zucchini noodles	Kale Chips (p.27); Raw crackers with Quick Pickled Onions (p.62) or sauerkraut
Buckwheat Cereal (p.107) with nut milk and berries	Red Pepper and Walnut Dip (p.165); Mixed salad; Herb and Tomato Flaxseed Crackers (p.148)	Raw pizza with salad; Creamy Coleslaw (p.69)	Water Kefir (p.197); Coconut Berry Chia Pudding (p.170)
Green juice; Soaked muesli (oats, nuts, and seeds soaked in nut milk overnight)	Kale salad with pumpkin seeds and cranberries	Asparagus and Broccoli Salad (p.72); Berry Cheesecake (p.112)	Superfruit Truffles (p.136); Orange Mango Nut Yogurt (p.116)

Is the Raw Food Diet Suitable for Everyone?

If you are considering following a raw food diet it is advisable to seek nutritional advice from a healthcare practitioner to make sure it is appropriate for you. A raw food diet can be nutritious and diverse, but it is important to ensure that it includes all the essential nutrients for optimal health and well-being. If you suffer with a long-term health condition and/or take medications then seek advice before making any major changes to your diet.

While a healthy raw food diet is perfectly safe it is not recommended to eat raw meat, fish, dairy, or eggs if you are pregnant or suffer with a compromised immune system. If you do consume raw meat, fish, eggs, and dairy it is essential to be confident of its quality and safety (see page 18). If you are pregnant it is equally important to ensure that you eat enough calories and get all the nutrients you need to support the growth of your baby (right).

There is no reason why children cannot follow a raw food based diet but make sure that it is balanced and nutrient rich to support their growth and development. Children also have high nutritional requirements and as certain nutrients can be low on a raw food diet,

supplementation may be necessary. Care should also be taken regarding food hygiene and safety especially if you are thinking about eating raw meat, fish, eggs, or dairy products.

Key Principles of a Healthy Raw Food Diet

1 Focus on Quality of Food
The raw food approach is not about quantity or calories but nutritional density of food. One of the best ways of ensuring this is to start eating organic, locally grown, seasonal fruit and vegetables, and organic nuts, seeds, and beans. This will maximize their nutritional content and minimize the exposure to toxins. Try to incorporate a range of nutrient rich superfoods into your diet to provide additional essential nutrients and focus on fresh, enzyme rich foods, such as avocados, rather than relying on dehydrated products.

2 Eat Enough Protein in Every Meal
Many people adopting a raw food diet are often low in protein. Ensure that each meal includes protein—this could include leafy greens, nuts, seeds, sprouted beans, and grains like quinoa, or certain superfoods and protein powders. Adequate protein is essential for many bodily processes and maintaining healthy muscle mass, which tends to decrease as we age.

3 Don't Be Afraid of Healthy Fats
One mistake some people following a raw food diet can make is to cut back on healthy fats. However, these are essential for your health and are a useful energy source for your body. Avoid processed refined vegetable oils and include whole foods that are rich in healthy fats such as coconut, avocado (as shown above), olives, nuts, and seeds.

4 Choose a Wide Range of Foods
There is a vast range of foods that can be included in the raw food diet. Each week aim to include a new food—by eating a greater variety you will ensure a diverse range of nutrients and antioxidants in your diet that will keep your body healthy.

5 Keep Dishes Simple

Don't overcomplicate dishes—by keeping it simple you focus on high quality ingredients and keep meals fresh and nutrient rich. A few good dressings can transform the simplest of dishes. Equally, blended green smoothies are easy to make and are packed with nutrients. If you do invest in a dehydrator you can also make batches of raw crackers and granolas to snack on when you are short on time.

6 Limit Natural Sugars

One of the temptations with a raw food diet is to overconsume fresh fruit, dried fruit, and sweeteners, such as honey and maple syrup. Sugar is inflammatory and promotes oxidative damage, which can lead to chronic diseases, tooth decay, and weight gain. If you suffer with blood sugar imbalances then you may also wish to limit your intake of fresh fruit to one to two portions a day and avoid dried fruits.

7 Include Fermented Foods

Foods containing healthy bacteria (probiotic foods) are essential for keeping our digestive systems healthy. One of the best ways to increase the levels of healthy microbes in your gut is to eat fermented or cultured foods daily. These include homemade nut yogurt (see page 116), like almond or coconut, kefir, sauerkraut, kimchi, and Kombucha (see page 158).

8 Keep Hydrated and Drink Water

Don't overlook the importance of fluids in your diet. Water is essential for digesting and absorbing foods, transporting nutrients around the body, keeping cells functioning properly, and removing toxins via the liver and kidneys. Not drinking enough can make you feel tired and lead to toxic buildup. One of the benefits of a raw food diet is that it is naturally hydrating. Eating fresh fruits and vegetables, green juices, and smoothies will contribute to your fluid intake. However, it is also important to include plenty of filtered water every day.

9 Start Sprouting

Sprouting nuts, seeds, beans, and grains (as shown below) greatly enhances their nutritional profile and makes them more readily digestible. By getting into the habit of sprouting you will increase your intake of protein and essential nutrients.

10 Be Flexible in Your Diet

It might be that you prefer to eat a partially raw diet for a length of time—for example 40–50 percent raw before advancing to almost fully raw. In some cases, you may never fully transition to a wholly raw food diet but mix it with 60 percent raw food and 40 percent vegan cooked food, for example. During the cooler months you may find that you need a greater intake of cooked foods. It is important to listen to your body and adjust your diet accordingly.

11 Eat Leafy Greens Every Day

Eating leafy green vegetables daily is highly recommended, as they are packed with lots of important nutrients and are alkalizing. Blending them into a smoothie (as shown below) is a quick and efficient way to cram more greens into your diet. Alternatively, eat a raw salad that includes leafy greens every day.

12 Eat Meals Mindfully

Take your time over meals. Rather than eating on the run, sit at a table and eat slowly and mindfully (as shown above). Doing so will promote healthy digestion, will slow down the release of glucose into the bloodstream keeping blood sugars more stable, and will make you less likely to overeat. Listen to your body and only eat if you are truly hungry. Many people following a raw food diet enjoy intermittent fasting focusing on green juices and smoothies to help with weight loss. Others who are very active find that they need regular snacks in addition to meals to fuel their workouts.

13 Don't Forget Lifestyle Changes

Optimal health is about being healthy in body, mind, and spirit. In addition to watching what you eat it's important to get adequate exercise, reduce stress, spend time outdoors, and surround yourself with supportive friends and family.

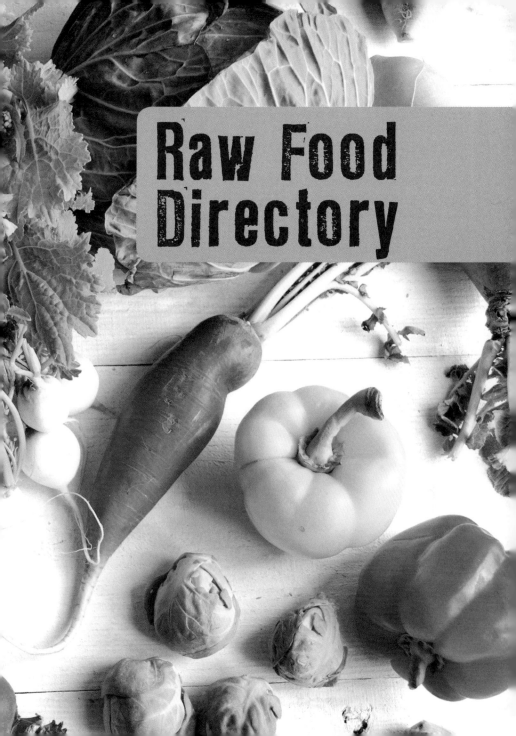

Raw Food Directory

Vegetables

Vegetables are an essential part of a raw food diet as they contain a huge range of phytonutrients, antioxidants, vitamins, minerals, and fiber, which are all necessary to keep the body healthy. Try to eat a wide selection of vegetables every day to keep you fit and healthy.

The diversity of phytonutrients present in many vegetables contributes to their health protective properties. Being potent antioxidants they help protect the body from the effects of harmful free radicals as well as helping to reduce inflammation, which is often a precursor to chronic diseases. Their fiber content is also important for supporting a healthy digestive system as well as regulating blood sugar levels. Certain vegetables are also rich in protein making them an important contribution in a raw food diet.

However, there are some vegetables that should not be eaten raw. Potatoes—particularly green ones—can have a high concentration of toxins known as solanine, an alkaloid. Similarly yucca, also known as cassava, should not be eaten raw.

As cruciferous and leafy green vegetables are particularly nutritious try to eat a minimum of one to two cups daily. These vegetables are also known for their potential cancer-fighting properties and detoxifying benefits so they are excellent for overall health and longevity.

Health Benefits of Vegetables

 Eye health: Many vegetables are good sources of vitamin A and the carotenoids lutein and zeaxanthin. Lutein and zeaxanthin are primary antioxidants that function in several regions of the eye, including the retina and macula. A diet rich in vegetables can help reduce the risk of age-related macular degeneration and cataracts. Vitamin A is also important for improving nighttime vision.

 Heart health: Leafy vegetables are rich in B vitamins, which lower homocysteine—an amino acid produced by the body—to help prevent strokes and heart attacks. They also contain magnesium to keep the heart healthy.

 Stress: Vegetables, especially green vegetables, provide lots of nutrients that help you cope with stress, tension, and anxiety, such as B vitamins, folate, omega-3 fatty acids, magnesium, potassium, and glutathione.

 Skin health: Vegetables hydrate your skin, which can reduce the appearance of wrinkles. Being rich in phytonutrients they help guard against aging by preventing cell damage from ultraviolet light and environmental toxins. Vegetables also contain good amounts of vitamin C which helps in the production of collagen, essential for a glowing skin.

 Bone health: Vegetables, particularly leafy greens, provide essential minerals for healthy bones including calcium, magnesium, vitamin K, and phosphorous.

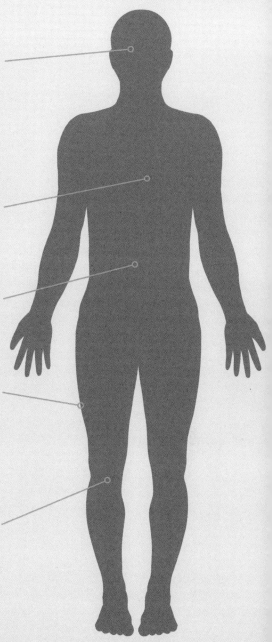

Leafy Greens and Brassicas

Leafy greens are incredibly rich in nutrients and should be a key feature in any raw food diet.

Packed with vitamins, minerals, and disease-fighting phytochemicals, leafy greens are known for their cancer-protective properties. They are also high in fiber, which helps with digestion, and are ideal to eat for weight loss and maintenance because they keep you feeling full and help control feelings of hunger. Leafy greens contain a lot of water to keep you hydrated and contribute to glowing skin and hair. They are also particularly rich in minerals including bioavailable calcium, magnesium, and folate, which help to reduce your risk of cardiovascular disease and improve memory. Leafy greens also supply essential omega-3 fatty acids and protein.

Nutrition: Leafy greens are very nutritious as they are full of vitamins, minerals, and phytochemicals.
Benefits: A good source of vitamin E, which protects skin from sun damage, and vitamin C that helps with aging.

Kale

One of the most nutritious greens, kale is a good source of protein and supplies all the essential amino acids our bodies need.

- Rich in vitamin A and loaded with lutein and zeaxanthin, important for keeping the eyes healthy.
- Kale contains iron, essential for energy.
- Per calorie, kale has more calcium than milk, which helps prevent osteoporosis.

Spinach

Spinach is a good source of antioxidants, including vitamin C, beta-carotene, lutein, and zeaxanthin, which helps to maintain healthy eyes, hair, and skin.

- Spinach contains high amounts of potassium and vitamin K, which can help to support the heart.
- A good source of iron and B vitamins to help with energy levels.

Broccoli

This cruciferous vegetable is packed with vitamin K, a nutrient that is essential for healthy bones.

- Broccoli contains the sulfur compound, sulforaphane, known for its cancer-protective properties.
- Packed with vitamin C, which helps in the production of collagen to keep the skin supple.

Cabbage

Cabbage and other cruciferous vegetables like cauliflower contain tumor-fighting compounds called glucosinolates, which inhibit the growth of cancerous cells, help with detoxfiying the colon, and boost the immune system.

- Cabbage juice has traditionally been used to relieve stomach ulcers and soothe the digestive tract.

Cauliflower

Low in calories, cauliflower makes a useful low carb alternative to rice. Grate or chop in a food processor to form grains then use as an alternative to couscous or rice. It can also be used in Nori Rolls (see page 78).

- Cauliflower contains sulfur compounds to support detoxification.
- A good source of choline, a B vitamin known for its role in memory.

Brussels Sprouts

Delicious shredded and tossed in a dressing for salads, Brussels sprouts are rich in glucosinolates, which have cancer-protective properties.

- Brussels sprouts are exceptionally high in nutrients including B vitamins, vitamin A, K, iron, magnesium, phosphorus, copper, and calcium, all good for maintaining a healthy heart.

Turnip Greens

Turnip greens are the tops of turnip bulbs, and are a delicious addition to raw salads and green juices.

- They are a good source of antioxidants including vitamins C and E, beta-carotene, lutein, and zeaxanthin to help support the immune system.
- Turnip greens are rich in iron, so are ideal to include in a raw food diet.

Watercress

Watercress is a leafy green vegetable with a spicy, peppery flavor.

- A rich source of beta-carotene, lutein, and zeaxanthin, antioxidants that may prevent and manage arthritis, cataracts, and maintain healthy hair and skin.
- Watercress contains isothiocyanates, compounds that have been shown to fight a range of cancers.

Collards

Collard greens are a cruciferous and leafy green vegetable, closely related to kale.

- Rich in vitamin K for healthy bones, collards can also help with memory by limiting neuronal damage in the brain.
- Collards are one of the best cruciferous vegetables for lowering cholesterol by binding bile in the digestive tract to make it easier to exit the body.

Bok Choy

Bok choy, also known as leafy Chinese cabbage, is an increasingly popular green.

- As a good source of vitamin C, vitamin A (carotenoids), manganese, and zinc, bok choy offers antioxidant protection and anti-inflammatory support.
- Bok choy contains omega-3 fatty acids such as alpha-linolenic acid (ALA), which is important for brain health.

Kale Salad with Pumpkin Seeds and Cranberries

HIGH FIBER

A healthy raw food diet is one based around plenty of green foods especially dark leafy greens such as kale. The kale leaves soften and wilt when mixed with the dressing ingredients giving it a cooked texture and creamy flavor.

Prep: 15 mins

Ingredients (serves 4)

14 oz (400 g) kale leaves
1 teaspoon garlic salt or sea salt
¼ cup (30 g) pumpkin seeds
½ cup (50 g) dried cranberries

Dressing

1 large ripe avocado
2 teaspoons tamari or coconut aminos
½ teaspoon onion powder
2 tablespoons flaxseed oil or olive oil
Drizzle of maple syrup
Juice of ½ lemon

Method

1 Wash the kale, remove any tough stalks, and chop into small pieces.

2 Add the salt and, using your hands, massage into the kale leaves squeezing them until the leaves begin to wilt.

3 Make the dressing by blending all the ingredients together in a blender or food processor to form a thick paste. Alternatively, mash the avocado in a bowl and mix in the remaining ingredients.

4 Pour the dressing over the kale and massage into the salad with your hands, making sure the kale is coated.

5 Add the pumpkin seeds and cranberries and toss in the kale. Serve at once.

PROMOTES HEALTHY SKIN AND BONES	
Calories (per serving)	245
Protein	6.5 g
Total fat	19.1 g
of which saturated fat	3.4 g
Carbohydrates	11.7 g
of which sugars	10.2 g
Vitamins/minerals	A, C, manganese, zinc

Swiss Chard

Swiss chard, also known as silverbeet, is low in calories and is one of the most nutritious leafy green vegetables available.

- An excellent source of calcium, magnesium, and vitamin K, which all help to maintain healthy bones.
- Swiss chard is rich in antioxidants, vitamins C, E, and A, manganese, and zinc, to help with increasing energy.

Radish

Known for their peppery taste, radishes are an effective detoxifying vegetable and diuretic increasing urine production.

- Radishes are rich in vitamin C and antioxidant anthocyanins that may inhibit cancer growth.
- They have a high water content which makes them helpful for maintaining healthy moisture levels in the skin.

Rapini

Rapini, also known as broccoli raab, is ideal to use in healthy green smoothies.

- Rapini contains powerful cancer-fighting phytochemicals and vitamin K, which is important for strengthening bones.
- A good source of folate and vitamin C, which helps to reduce homocysteine, an amino acid that damages arteries.

Concerned About Goitrogens?

Cruciferous vegetables belong to the Brassicaceae family. They are also known as Cruciferae (meaning "cross-bearing") because the four petals in their flowers resemble a cross shape. They include cauliflower, cabbage, garden cress, bok choy, broccoli, Brussels sprouts, arugula, collards, and other green leafy vegetables.

Goitrogens are compounds found in cruciferous vegetables, and some other vegetables and fruits, that can cause the enlargement of the thyroid gland and prevent the thyroid getting its necessary amount of iodine.

Iodine is an essential mineral for the production of the thyroid hormones T4 (thyroxine) and T3 (triiodothyronine). Those with Hashimoto's or Grave's disease (autoimmune thyroid conditions) or hypothyroidism are sometimes advised to avoid eating raw cruciferous vegetables for this reason. However, there is little scientific research to suggest that consumption of these vegetables will cause a decrease in thyroid function in the absence of iodine deficiency. If you do have a thyroid condition eat iodine rich foods, such as sea vegetables (see page 74) regularly. Make sure your diet is rich in the necessary minerals for thyroid hormone production, especially iodine, iron, selenium, and zinc, and don't eat too many cruciferous vegetables. Cooking reduces the goitrogen levels so if you are concerned about your thyroid function you may wish to lightly steam or blanch cruciferous vegetables rather than eating them raw. As cruciferous vegetables are nutritious, they should form a significant part of your diet.

Why Eat Lettuce?

There are various types of lettuce, but all of them are low in calories and a good source of fiber, making them excellent for losing weight. As well as using them in salads, lettuce can be added to green smoothies, juices, and the leaves of varieties such as Boston make wonderful wraps for raw falafels and burgers. You can also blend lettuce with different spices and coconut cream or avocado to make a delicious creamy raw soup. Always buy organic lettuce to get the most nutrients and reduce exposure to harmful chemicals.

- Some types of lettuce, such as romaine and butterhead, are good sources of antioxidants, including beta-carotene, lutein, zeaxanthin, and quercetin, which have anti-inflammatory benefits.
- Lettuce is also a good source of potassium, which helps in managing blood pressure and regulating fluid balance, as well as vitamin K, which is important for healthy bones.

Lamb's Lettuce

Lamb's lettuce has small, delicate leaves that make an ideal addition to salads.

- Lamb's lettuce is a good source of beta-carotene, which is converted by the body into vitamin A to prevent night blindness and maintain healthy skin.
- This lettuce is a useful source of calcium and vitamin C to strengthen blood vessel walls.

Arugula

A leafy green vegetable with a peppery taste, arugula is often used in salads.

- Arugula is rich in vitamins A and C for a healthy immune system.
- A good source of certain phytochemicals, such as indoles, thiocyanates, sulforaphane, and iso-thiocyanates, known for their anticancer benefits and detoxification support.

Mustard Greens

Mustard greens come from the mustard plant and have a peppery flavor.

- Mustard greens are packed with vitamin C, beta-carotene, lutein, and zeaxanthin, which are good for keeping the eyes and immune system healthy.
- Mustard greens are rich in folate, important for a healthy heart.
- They are high in fiber to aid digestion.

Radicchio

Radicchio, sometimes called Italian chicory, is a leafy vegetable with a bitter taste. For this reason it can be helpful in stimulating digestive secretions and improving digestion, as well as cleansing the colon due to its high fiber content.

- Radicchio is a good source of potassium and vitamin E to help support cell membranes and a healthy skin.

Romaine Lettuce

Romaine lettuce is a low-calorie, high-fiber, nutrient-rich vegetable to support a healthy weight and aid digestion.

- Romaine lettuce contains protein, omega-3 fatty acids, iron, and calcium.
- This lettuce also contains B vitamins to support energy and a healthy heart.
- Rich in vitamin K and magnesium, which are good for healthy bones.

Endive

Endive is a bitter leafy vegetable often used in salads or served as a side dish. There are lots of varieties including Belgian endive, escarole, and curly endive (frisée). Endive is very low in calories, which makes it a great addition to any weight-loss plan.

- Endive is a good source of potassium to help manage blood pressure and prevent osteoporosis.

Red Oak Leaf Lettuce

This lettuce is easily recognized by its loose clump of leaves tinged with shades of red to dark reddish-purple.

- Red oak leaf lettuce is an excellent source of carotenoids, which the body converts to vitamin A to support healthy skin, eyes, and immune system.
- This lettuce also contains vitamin K, essential for the nervous system.

Lettuce, Cucumber, and Mint Soup

CLEANSING

This is a deliciously soothing and creamy soup packed with lots of minerals and antioxidants. Incredibly hydrating, this is fabulous as a light lunch with raw crackers (see page 148).

Prep: 10 mins

Ingredients (serves 4)

½ romaine lettuce, chopped

2 cucumbers, chopped

1 tablespoon chopped fresh mint

1 teaspoon lime juice

½ teaspoon sea salt to taste

1 garlic clove

1 ripe avocado, peeled, pitted, and
   chopped

Drizzle of olive oil

Freshly ground black pepper

Method

1 Place all the ingredients in a blender and process until smooth. Season with pepper. Chill in the refrigerator, then serve garnished with cucumber and mint.

GREAT FOR A HEALTHY SKIN	
Calories (per serving)	72
Protein	2.0 g
Total fat	5.5 g
of which saturated fat	1.1 g
Carbohydrates	3.3 g
of which sugars	2.8 g
Vitamins/minerals	A, C, K₁, folate

Vegetable Fruits

A number of different fruits are considered vegetables as they are not particularly sweet and lend themselves to more savory dishes. Botanically, they are fruits as they contain seeds. They are also packed with vitamins, minerals, and antioxidants. Some, such as olives, are a good source of healthy monounsaturated fats.

Nutrition: Vegetable fruits are packed with nutrition including a variety of beneficial phytochemicals.
Benefits: High in fiber, so good for weight loss, vegetable fruits also have antiaging and anticancer properties.

Cucumber

Cucumbers belong to the Cucurbitaceae family, the same plant family as squash, pumpkin, and watermelon. Cucumbers are made up of 95 percent water, which makes them incredibly hydrating.

- Cucumbers are rich in antioxidants including vitamin C, flavonoids, beta-carotene, and B vitamins to help with stress levels and reduce anxiety.

Tomato

A good source of vitamins A, C, K, folate, and potassium, all important nutrients to keep the heart healthy.

- Tomatoes are ideal for maintaining a healthy skin as they are rich in beta-carotene and lycopene that help protect the skin against sun damage.
- Lycopene is also good for healthy bones as well as male fertility.

Bell Pepper

Green and purple bell peppers have a slightly bitter flavor, while the red, orange, and yellow varieties are sweeter and almost fruity.

- An excellent source of antioxidants, including vitamin C and carotenoids, together with sulfur compounds, peppers are good for cancer protection and help with detoxification.

Eggplant

Eggplants belong to the nightshade family of vegetables, which also includes tomatoes, sweet peppers, and potatoes.

- Rich in phytonutrients and flavonoids, to protect our cells from damage.
- Eggplants are packed with B vitamins and manganese to help boost energy.
- They are high in fiber so excellent for aiding weight loss.

Zucchini

Zucchini are high in antioxidants to help reduce inflammation.

- Rich in magnesium and potassium, which help normalize blood pressure.
- Packed with vitamin C and carotenoids to protect fats from being damaged.
- The skin is rich in carotenoids. Wax can be applied to the skin of nonorganic varieties so try to eat organic.

Why Eat Avocado?

A low-carbohydrate fruit, avocados are rich in monounsaturated fats that help to protect the heart. With more potassium than bananas they are also helpful for supporting healthy blood pressure levels.

- Avocados are high in fiber which helps stabilize blood sugar levels.
- They contain plenty of antioxidants, including lutein and zeaxanthin, which are important for keeping the eyes healthy and lower the risk of macular degeneration and cataracts.

Olives

While recognized as a high fat food, the majority of the fat found in olives is healthy monounsaturated fat.

- Olives contain lots of antioxidant phytonutrients and vitamin E. The combination of nutrients makes olives beneficial for their anti-inflammatory and anticancer properties, as well as improving the appearance of wrinkles.

Citrus Chili Guacamole

ENERGIZING

Rich and creamy with a lovely tang from the lime juice—
serve this guacamole with vegetable sticks, raw crackers
(see page 148), or as a topping for raw burgers and falafels.

Prep: 8 mins

Ingredients (serves 4)

2 ripe avocados

2 tablespoons lime juice

½ teaspoon Himalayan salt

2 tomatoes, diced

½ red chili, seeded and diced

1 teaspoon ground cumin

1 garlic clove, crushed, optional

Small handful of cilantro leaves, chopped

Method

1 Mash the avocados in a bowl, add the remaining ingredients, and mix well. Season to taste and serve at once.

PROMOTES A HEALTHY HEART	
Calories (per serving)	102
Protein	1.3 g
Total fat	9.9 g
of which saturated fat	2.1 g
Carbohydrates	2.0 g
of which sugars	1.3 g
Vitamins/minerals	C, potassium, folate

Squashes

Summer and winter squashes are fruits and are relatives of the melon and cucumber. There are many different varieties and all can be eaten raw. Summer varieties like zucchini are ideal used in salads or spiralized to create noodles. Winter squashes have hard shells and their seeds are a good source of omega-3 fatty acids.

Nutrition: Squashes are very nutritious and are high in vitamins A, C, B, and omega-3 fatty acids.
Benefits: They keep the heart healthy, regulate blood sugar levels, and are powerful anti-inflammatories.

Pumpkin

Pumpkins are delicious in smoothies, desserts, or raw crackers (see page 148).

- An excellent source of vitamin A and carotenoids, which is good for keeping the skin and eyes healthy.
- Pumpkins are valued for their cancer-protective benefits.
- They have anti-inflammatory properties, helpful for postexercise soreness.

Butternut Squash

Shaped like a large pear, this squash has a sweet flavor. Butternut squash is ideal for using in salads and smoothies, or blended into raw cheesecakes and tarts.

- Butternut squash contain high levels of vitamins A, C, and E, which protects against cell damage.
- This squash contains potassium for maintaining healthy blood pressure.

Kabocha Squash

A type of Japanese squash that is becoming increasingly popular in the United States, kabocha is very sweet in flavor.

- A rich source of beta-carotene, which is converted by the body to vitamin A to keep the eyes, skin, and hair healthy.
- This squash is a good source of iron, vitamin C, and certain B vitamins to help with energy and adrenal health.

Spaghetti Squash

Spaghetti squash gets its name from the fact that when it is cooked the inside flesh pulls out of the shell in long strands, resembling spaghetti pasta. This makes it a great alternative to noodles.

- Spaghetti squash is a good source of antioxidants, B vitamins, vitamin C, potassium, and manganese, making it a wonderful energizing food.

Acorn Squash

Acorn squash is so named because when fully grown, aside from its green color, it looks quite similar to large acorns.

- Packed with fiber, acorn squash can help digestion, detoxification, and regulate blood sugar levels.
- This squash is also rich in potassium, magnesium, manganese, iron, copper, phosphorous, and calcium.

Onions

Alliums (also known as the onion family) are known for their powerful aroma. Onions have been used medicinally for hundreds of years. They were eaten by the Roman emperor Nero as a cure for the common cold and for centuries were used in folk medicine for the relief of coughs, colds, and catarrh, especially asthma. More recently some of their curative properties have been attributed to a compound called allyl propyl disulfide, which may improve detoxification, keep the immune system healthy, keep connective tissue strong, and balance blood sugar levels.

To maximize the health benefits of onions it is best to eat them raw as they contain organic sulfur compounds in a

Nutrition: Onions contain phytochemicals which make vitamin C in the body work more efficiently.
Benefits: Onions regulate blood sugar, reduce inflammation, help heal infections, and soothe coughs.

volatile oil, which are partly destroyed by heat from cooking. However, not everyone finds raw onions easy to digest. To improve digestibility try marinating or pickling them (see page 62). Alternatively, blend a small amount of raw onion into raw crackers (see page 148). With their unique combination of flavonoids and sulfur-containing nutrients, the allium vegetables should be a regular part of your raw food diet.

Red Onion

Sweet tasting and mild in flavor, red onions are delicious in salads or blended into raw burgers or falafels to provide extra flavor.

- Red onions are packed with quercetin, a bioflavonoid known for its anti-inflammatory and anticancer properties.
- Onions are a good source of biotin, a B vitamin known for keeping the hair in good condition.

White Onion

The high sulfur content in white onions may help to strengthen connective tissue and bone, and keep blood free from clots.

- White onions are high in sulfur-containing nutrients, which are useful in detoxifying the body of heavy metals.
- They are a good source of manganese, copper, and B vitamins, all of which are good for energy.

Leek

Milder in flavor than onions, leeks are an ideal addition to salads and raw soups.

- Leeks contain a range of phytonutrients including the flavonoid kaempferol, known for its anti-inflammatory benefits, which helps to protect the blood vessel linings from damage.
- Packed with other vitamins that are important for improving memory.

Quick Pickled Onions

LOW CALORIE

These onions are a wonderful accompaniment to homemade raw burgers, wraps, and salads. This is a quick and easy recipe that will work well with both red and white onions. Vary the flavorings according to taste. Store in the refrigerator for two to three weeks.

Prep: 10 mins/Pickle: 30 mins

Ingredients (serves 4)

1 teaspoon coconut sugar
½ teaspoon sea salt
Generous ¾ cup (200 ml) rice vinegar, white wine vinegar, or apple cider vinegar
1 small garlic clove, halved
5 black peppercorns
5 allspice berries
1 red onion, halved and thinly sliced

Method

1 Preheat the oven to 275°F (140°C, gas mark 1). Sterilize a pickling jar by washing in hot soapy water, rinsing, and placing in the oven to dry completely.

2 Add the sugar, salt, vinegar, and flavorings to the jar and stir or shake to dissolve.

3 Place the sliced onions in a bowl and pour over boiling water. Leave for 1 minute then drain. Add the onions to the jar and stir well to combine the flavorings.

4 Let the onions pickle for at least 30 minutes. The flavor will improve if the pickle is left for several hours. Store in the refrigerator until needed.

HELPS TO BOOST YOUR IMMUNE SYSTEM	
Calories (per serving)	30
Protein	0.7 g
Total fat	0.1 g
of which saturated fat	0.0 g
Carbohydrates	4.4 g
of which sugars	3.2 g
Vitamins/minerals	C, B$_6$, manganese

Garlic

Garlic is rich in the antifungal sulfur compound called allicin that is responsible for its distinctive smell.

- Garlic supplementation has been shown to lower total and LDL cholesterol, improve blood pressure, and strengthen the immune system.
- Garlic contains antioxidants to help combat aging.

Scallion

Scallions, sometimes called green onions, are usually used in raw Chinese and Thai-inspired dishes and salads.

- Scallions are loaded with vitamins C and K, both of which are essential for the normal functioning of bones. Vitamin C helps in the synthesis of collagen—an important protein for bones, while vitamin K improves bone density.

Chives

Mild in flavor, chives make a great addition to raw dishes.

- Chives contain a high amount of vitamin K, an important vitamin to limit neuronal damage in the brain.
- High in fiber, chives can help aid digestion and prevent constipation.
- Chives also contain iron, calcium, magnesium, potassium, and B vitamins.

Root Vegetables

Root vegetables are incredibly high in nutrients. As they grow underground their nutritional profile will be influenced by the quality of the soil they are grown in so it is important to buy good quality organic produce where possible. Root vegetables contain antioxidants, vitamins C, B, A, and iron to help keep the body energized.

Nutrition: Root vegetables are high in vitamins and minerals that they absorb from the ground.

Benefits: High in fiber, low in fat, and high in complex carbohydrates, which give energy when broken down.

Carrot

A popular root vegetable, carrots are known for their high beta-carotene content, which is converted into vitamin A in the liver.

- Carrots contain vitamin A, which is vital to keep the immune system, skin, and eyes healthy.
- They are a rich source of vitamin K to keep bones healthy.

Sweet Potato

Sweet potatoes can be used to make dehydrated chips, or blended into soups and smoothies.

- Sweet potatoes are known for their high levels of carotenoids, ideal for lowering inflammation and helping with postexercise recovery.
- They are a good source of vitamin E to protect against heart disease.

Beets

Beets are valued for their help in detoxifiying the body and purifying the blood and liver.

- Drinking beet juice may help to lower blood pressure. This is because they are high in nitric oxide, which relaxes and dilates the blood vessels improving blood flow, and may also help to improve physical stamina.

Parsnip

Parsnips are delicious grated or processed to form "rice" which can then be used to make raw Nori Rolls (see page 78), or to replace rice in dishes.

- Parsnips are good for keeping the heart healthy as they are rich in potassium, which acts as a vasodilator and reduces blood pressure.
- They are high in fiber to aid digestion.

Rutabaga

Mild and sweet in flavor, rutabaga is low in carbohydrate and often used grated into raw salads and coleslaw.

- Rutabaga contains vitamins C and A, to keep the immune system healthy.
- Good source of calcium, potassium, and zinc, important for the heart and bones.
- They have a good amount of fiber to help aid digestion.

Beet Chips

LOW CALORIE

These delicious crispy snacks make a wonderful alternative to potato chips. Dehydrate them until crispy and keep in an airtight container. You can vary the spices according to taste. If you don't have a dehydrator bake them in a very low oven until crisp.

Prep: 5 mins/Marinate: 10 mins
Dry: 24 hrs

Ingredients (serves 4)

4 tablespoons apple cider vinegar
1 tablespoon olive oil
Pinch of smoked paprika, or to taste
2 tablespoons water
4 raw beets—you could use golden and
    red varieties for color, very thinly sliced
Himalayan sea salt and freshly ground
    black pepper

Method

1 Mix the vinegar, oil, spice, and water together. Place the beets in the vinegar mixture and marinate for 10 minutes.

2 Spread the beet out on nonstick sheets and season. Dehydrate at 115°F (46°C) for 24 hours or until crispy.

PACKED WITH ANTIOXIDANTS	
Calories (per serving)	59
Protein	1.8 g
Total fat	2.4 g
of which saturated fat	0.3 g
Carbohydrates	7.2 g
of which sugars	6.7 g
Vitamins/minerals	C, folate, potassium

Turnip

Choose smaller, baby turnips for their delicate, sweet flavor.

- A good source of B vitamins, turnips help to keep the skin, eyes, and hair healthy.
- Turnips contain calcium for healthy bones, muscles, and the nervous system.
- Rich in sulfur compounds and indoles, which may inhibit cancer cell growth.

Kohlrabi

Also known as German turnip or turnip cabbage, kohlrabi is a tasty and versatile variety of cabbage.

- Kohlrabi contains glucosinolates, which are known for their cancer-protective and detoxification benefits.
- A good source of vitamin C, kohlrabi helps to keep skin and bones healthy due to its antioxidant properties.

Fennel

Fennel belongs to the Umbellifereae family and is closely related to parsley, carrots, dill, and cilantro.

- Rich in phytonutrients, particularly anethole, which is known to reduce inflammation and help prevent cancer.
- Fennel is a good source of vitamin C, folate, potassium, and fiber to help with the excretion of cholesterol and toxins.

Creamy Coleslaw

HIGH FIBER

This is a delicious way to make the most of root vegetables. The dressing is made with tahini or sesame seed paste which is rich in calcium and magnesium. You can also use this dressing over salads for a creamy texture. Vary the vegetables according to taste.

Prep: 10 mins

Ingredients (serves 4)

1 carrot, grated or cut into julienne

7 oz (200 g) kohlrabi, cut into julienne

4 oz (125 g) white cabbage, shredded

1 small white onion, minced

Dressing

3 tablespoons tahini (sesame seed paste)

3 tablespoons water

1 tablespoon Dijon mustard, or to taste

2 teaspoons maple syrup, coconut syrup,
　　or honey

2 teaspoons apple cider vinegar

Salt and freshly ground black pepper

Method

1 Make the dressing by whisking all the ingredients together.

2 Place all the vegetables in a bowl and toss in the dressing. Season to taste.

CLEANSING AND CAN HELP WEIGHT LOSS	
Calories (per serving)	121
Protein	4.3 g
Total fat	7.4 g
of which saturated fat	1.1 g
Carbohydrates	8.9 g
of which sugars	8.3 g
Vitamins/minerals	C, K₁, folate, thiamin

Other Vegetables

There are many other vegetables that provide the body with lots of nutrients, are low in calories and fat, high in fiber, and also add further variety to your diet, such as celery, peas, and asparagus. Aim to include as wide a range of vegetables in your daily diet as you possibly can to help keep your body fit and healthy.

Nutrition: Vegetables are packed with many nutrients including potassium, vitamins A, C, and E, and lots of fiber.
Benefits: Eating a diet rich in a variety of vegetables may reduce the risk of heart disease and strokes.

Celery

A popular ingredient in green juices, celery is a low-calorie high-fiber food perfect to support a healthy weight.

- Packed with vitamin C, potassium, iron, and folate.
- Celery has a high water and fiber content and crunchy texture, which are not only ideal for helping you feel satisfied, but ensure that you stay fuller for longer.

Asparagus

Packing around half its calories from protein, this is an ideal vegan vegetable to support healthy muscle mass.

- Asparagus is high in vitamin A, folate, and fiber, which are all thought to play a vital role in fighting cancer.
- Containing high levels of potassium, asparagus helps support healthy blood pressure and fluid balance in the body.

Okra

Also known as ladies' fingers, okra is a popular vegetable in Asian dishes.

- Studies suggest okra may help improve blood sugar levels.
- Okra is also rich in fiber and may help lower cholesterol and improve digestion.
- Contains vitamin K for bone health.
- Okra is packed with B vitamins and iron to improve energy levels.

Peas

Green peas provide a good source of protein and fiber, which may help with regulating blood sugar. Pea sprouts are also incredibly nutritious and are a good source of antioxidants and vitamin C.

- Peas contain a number of disease-fighting compounds known for their anticancer properties.

Corn

The different colors of corn contain a wide range of potent phytonutrients. Yellow corn is rich in carotenoids, blue corn is packed with anthocyanin antioxidants, while purple corn contains protocatechuic acid, which is known for its strong antioxidant activity.

- Corn is rich in B vitamins and fiber, to help support a healthy digestive system.

Asparagus and Broccoli Salad

CLEANSING

This is a light refreshing spring salad packed with nutrients and fiber. Simply toss in a little lemon juice, capers, and olive oil or, for a spicy kick, serve with this delicious light Japanese-style dressing.

Prep: 10 mins

Ingredients (serves 4)

7 oz (200 g) broccoli florets
8 thin asparagus spears, trimmed
2¼ oz (60 g) sugar snap peas
2 large handfuls of mixed salad greens
Sea salt

Dressing

2 tablespoons miso paste
½ garlic clove, crushed
3 tablespoons mirin
1 tablespoon coconut sugar or xylitol
2 teaspoons tamari soy sauce or
     coconut aminos
1 teaspoon grated fresh ginger root
3 tablespoons rice wine vinegar
4 tablespoons olive oil
Salt and freshly ground black pepper

Method

1 Cut the broccoli into small florets and slice the asparagus spears into small lengths. Place in a salad bowl with the sugar snap peas and salad greens and toss in a little sea salt.

2 Whisk all the ingredients for the dressing together then drizzle the dressing over the salad to serve.

EXCELLENT FOR A HEALTHY HEART	
Calories (per serving)	136
Protein	4.5 g
Total fat	10.1 g
of which saturated fat	1.4 g
Carbohydrates	7.3 g
of which sugars	1.7 g
Vitamins/minerals	K₁, B₆, iron, thiamin

Sea Vegetables

Sea vegetables (or seaweeds) are among the oldest living species on earth and have been eaten in Asian countries for centuries. As ocean water is rich in minerals one of the particular benefits of eating sea vegetables is to replenish dietary minerals that are essential for our health. For vegans and those following a raw food diet they are one of nature's best sources of vegetable protein and provide abundant antioxidants including beta-carotene, chlorophyll, and fiber. They also provide omega-3 fatty acids, are exceptionally rich in vitamins and minerals, and provide one of the few plant based sources of B₁₂.

Sea vegetables contain fucoidans, which may explain why these vegetables have many health benefits. Fucoidans are starchlike sulfur-containing molecules or polysaccharides. Known for their anti-inflammatory benefits they appear to help the proper functioning of the immune system and promote cardiovascular health. Available in various forms—dried, flakes, or powdered—many varieties of sea vegetables need soaking in water for five to ten minutes before using. Sea vegetables have traditionally been eaten in moderate amounts and on a regular basis to provide a balanced intake of minerals.

Sea vegetables are one of the most abundant source of iodine, a mineral that is

Nutrition: Sea vegetables are high in fiber, provide a good range of essential minerals, and are low in calories.

Benefits: A diet rich in sea vegetables reduces the risk of some diseases and helps the body eliminate toxins.

typically low in people's diet. Iodine helps with memory, a healthy thyroid gland, metabolism, and may reduce the risk of certain cancers, such as breast cancer.

Sea vegetables act like a filter in the oceans where they grow so source them carefully and only buy organic varieties.

Each of the sea vegetables has a distinct flavor and are ideal to use in raw soups, salads, raw crackers (see page 148), wraps, and dips.

Sea Vegetable Mixes

If you are new to sea vegetables then one of the best ways of including them in your diet is to use a mix. These contain a variety of sea vegetables including wakame, nori, and arame. Soak in water for five minutes then drain. Mixes are ideal for adding to salads. Sea vegetables are also high in lignans, plant substances that become phytoestrogens in the body, which can be helpful for balancing female hormones.

Dulse

Red or purple in color, dulse is rich in iodine and minerals, particularly phosphorous, iron, and potassium. It is available as flakes, which can be sprinkled over dishes before serving, or rehydrated and tossed into raw soups and salads.

- A good source of protein and also high in fiber that helps to cleanse the colon and improve digestion and absorption.

Nori

Best known as the outer wrap for sushi, nori is an edible red seaweed popular in East Asia, especially Japan. Available as dried sheets, toasted strips, flakes, or powder, it can be used to make raw sushi rolls (see page 78), or add to soups and raw crackers.

- Provides protein, omega-3 fatty acids, and is a good source of iron and calcium.

Hijiki

Hijiki is available in a twiglike dried form. It has a stronger flavor with aniselike undertones. Some studies have shown that it can contain high levels of arsenic, so eat it in small amounts, only buy organic, and prepare it according to the package directions to reduce the arsenic content.

- Hijiki is useful if watching your weight as it is high in fiber and low in calories.

Wakame

Wakame is an edible brown seaweed common in Japanese, Korean, and Chinese cooking. Soak for 15 minutes until soft, then drain, rinse, and add to salads.

- Rich in magnesium and calcium for healthy bones.
- Wakame is rich in alginate, a starch, which slows down digestion and makes food release its energy more slowly.

Arame

An edible brown seaweed rich in iodine, making it good for metabolism and a healthy thyroid. Before use, soak for ten minutes in cold water; drain, rinse, and chop into small pieces, if desired.

- Arame, like other sea vegetables, is known to bind heavy metals and toxins and remove them from the body.
- Rich in fiber, it helps lower cholesterol.

Sea Kelp

You'll generally find kelp in its dried form; soaking it for several minutes makes it pliable and edible. Kelp also comes in a granulated form to be used instead of salt or as a mineral supplement to add to food.

- Kelp is an abundant source of vitamins and minerals like potassium, magnesium, calcium, and iron, perfect for keeping hair and skin healthy.

Kelp Noodles

Made from sea kelp, these noodles contain virtually no starches and only six calories per 4-oz (115-g) serving. A mineral-rich food, you can use them to make noodle salads or add them to soups. Neutral in taste, they work well with Asian sauces.

- Kelp noodles contain a wealth of minerals including iodine, iron, calcium, magnesium, and potassium.

Irish Moss

Irish moss, also known as carrageen moss, is popular in raw food dishes, acting as a thickener and binding agent. It grows along the rocky Atlantic coasts of Europe and North America and softens into a jellylike substance when warmed in liquid.

- Irish moss is rich in a range of minerals including iodine, magnesium, calcium, manganese, and zinc.

Sea Palm

Sea palm is a very popular sea vegetable as it has a sweet succulent taste, and is delicious in raw salads.

- Sea palm contains lots of minerals, including potassium to help maintain healthy blood pressure levels.
- High in fiber and protein, sea palm is effective for maintaining a healthy weight and balancing blood sugar levels.

Nori Rolls with Sushi Rice and Sweet Dipping Sauce

LOW CALORIE

Sushi is a wonderful treat and this raw version is simple and easy to prepare. For the filling use a range of vegetable strips according to taste. This recipe uses parsnip instead of the usual sushi rice, but cauliflower would work equally well.

Prep: 20 mins

Ingredients (serves 4)

1 parsnip, peeled and coarsely chopped
1¾ tablespoons pine nuts
½ teaspoon sea salt
1 tablespoon lemon juice
2 teaspoons tahini (sesame seed paste)
4 nori sheets
1 red bell pepper, cut into thin strips
¼ cucumber, peeled and julienned
1 carrot, julienned
Handful of alfalfa sprouts
Freshly ground black pepper

Dipping Sauce

2 tablespoons Chinese rice vinegar
2 teaspoons maple syrup, coconut syrup,
   or yacon syrup
1 or 2 teaspoons lime juice
½ teaspoon grated fresh ginger root
Dash of Tabasco sauce, or to taste
Salt and freshly ground black pepper

Method

1 To make the dipping sauce, whisk all the ingredients together in a bowl and season to taste. Set aside.

2 Make the parsnip rice. Place the parsnip, pine nuts, lemon juice, and tahini in a food processor and process to form ricelike grains. Place the mixture in a bowl and season with a little salt and black pepper, then set aside.

3 Place a nori sheet shiny side down on a rolling mat. Spread an even layer of the rice across the sheet on the bottom third closest to you and press down firmly. Place a line of pepper, cucumber, carrot, and a few alfalfa sprouts. Dampen the edges of the nori sheet with a little water and roll up tightly using the mat to help you. Cut into rolls with a serrated knife and serve with the dipping sauce.

GOOD FOR WEIGHT LOSS	
Calories (per serving)	96
Protein	2.6 g
Total fat	4.7 g
of which saturated fat	0.5 g
Carbohydrates	10.1 g
of which sugars	6.7 g
Vitamins/minerals	A, C, K, potassium

Superfoods

While there is no agreed definition of "superfoods" they are considered to be natural foods containing exceptionally high levels of nutrients, such as phytonutrients and antioxidants. Many do not only contain plenty of nutrients, they are also able to restore balance in the body.

Calorie per calorie superfoods contain a vast array of nutrients to help keep the body fit and healthy when compared to other fresh and processed foods. Much of our everyday processed foods are little more than empty calories devoid of nutrients. A superfood, in comparison, can often be relatively low in calories but packed with beneficial nutrients. This makes them an excellent choice for people wishing to improve their health and vitality.

By including superfoods in your daily diet you can increase your intake of essential nutrients quickly and naturally. Whether you're aiming to improve muscle tone, energize your body, boost mental and physical performance, feel radiant, or support your immune system, there is a superfood to help you. Superfoods are known as functional foods—that is they support the function and balance of body systems. These superfoods are not new. In fact, many have been eaten by indigenous cultures for thousands of years and have a long history of therapeutic use. Chia seeds, for example, have been enjoyed for centuries by ancient cultures throughout Central America as a food and a medicine. Although today we might think of them as a new and exciting discovery, these superfoods were once everyday staples.

Since superfoods are a very concentrated source of nutrients they only need to be used in small amounts—this makes them ideal for adding to foods and drinks, such as smoothies and juices, on a daily basis.

Health Benefits of Superfoods

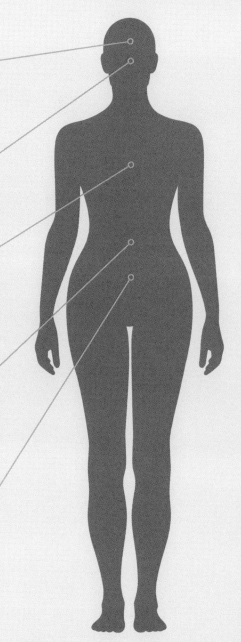

Brain health: Many superfood herbs are rich in antioxidants to protect brain cells and contain adaptogenic compounds (they enhance endurance) that can improve focus and concentration, and help to reduce anxiety.

Stress: Many superfoods—particularly herbs—are potent adaptogens, which help the body deal with everyday stress, as well as keep the adrenals and thyroid functioning well, and restoring hormonal balance.

Healthy aging: Superfoods are packed with antiaging antioxidants to protect cells from damage, which can contribute to aging and chronic diseases. Many are traditionally used to promote strength and resilience and are used as a tonic for improving the immune system.

Immune system: Many superfoods are rich in polysaccharides and antioxidants known to keep the immune system healthy, and possess antiviral and antimicrobial properties. Other superfoods help to strengthen and tone the body to make it more resilient to infections.

Detoxification: In particular, green superfoods are packed with chlorophyll and fiber known to support detoxification, alkalize the body, neutralize toxins, and eliminate them from the body. Some superfoods like milk thistle are also known to protect and help the liver.

Supergreens

Supergreens include algae, grasses, and herbs. Algae—single-celled organisms—are often considered to be a near-perfect food with an exceptionally high chlorophyll content. Grasses, such as wheatgrass, are equally rich in chlorophyll. It is this nutrient that gives supergreens their powerful cleansing and restorative properties.

Nutrition: Supergreens are packed with vitamins, minerals, enzymes, chlorophyll, and are high in protein.
Benefits: Help boost the immune system, detoxify the body, aid digestion, and reduce inflammation.

Spirulina

A type of blue-green algae, spirulina grows in warm, fresh water. It is thousands of years older than chlorella (see below) and does not have the same hard cell wall. Spirulina can be bought as a powder.

- Being incredibly high in protein—containing 65–71 percent—makes spirulina important for raw food diets.
- Spirulina contains vital amino acids.

Chlorella

Chlorella is a single-celled freshwater algae with a hard outer cell wall. Chlorella also contains complete proteins—in fact, it is made up of 50 percent protein. Buy as a powder or tablets, and choose cracked-cell-wall chlorella to ensure it is digestible.

- Chlorella is abundant in vitamins and minerals, including iron and B vitamins, needed for energy.

Moringa Leaf

Leaves from the moringa tree have been used for more than 2,000 years for their healing and nutritive value, as well as for their energy boost.

- Moringa leaf contains all the essential amino acids, making it a useful source of protein.
- Packed with antioxidants, including carotenoids and polyphenols, and a variety of vitamins, notably the B vitamins and vitamins A, C, E, and K.
- This supergreen is very high in calcium.

Green Tea and Matcha

Green and black tea come from the same plant, but green tea is the least processed and provides the most antioxidant polyphenols. Notably it provides a catechin, called epigallocatechin-3-gallate (EGCG), which is believed to be responsible for most of its health benefits, and has been shown to be effective at eliminating harmful free radicals. Matcha is green tea leaves that have been carefully ground to form a fine powder.

- Green tea has been shown to boost fat burning and metabolism, making it ideal for aiding weight loss.
- Matcha tea also contains the amino acid L-theanine, which stimulates the production of alpha brain waves to create a feeling of calm and alertness.

Why Eat Grasses?

Sprouted grasses and seeds, such as wheatgrass, sunflower sprouts, pea sprouts, broccoli sprouts, and barley grass, are well known for their cleansing and energizing properties. Wheatgrass is particularly popular due to its mild taste and exceptionally high content of chlorophyll. Sprouted grasses are alkalizing and energizing. The high chlorophyll content helps to oxygenate and cleanse the body to eliminate toxins.

Grasses are generally gluten free as it is only the grass that is used and not the seeds. However, if you are gluten intolerant check that the grasses have been processed in a certified gluten-free environment as some factories may handle products that contain gluten. Wheatgrass can be grown at home and juiced or it is available as a powder. Wheatgrass should be harvested at the jointing stage—as the young stems just start to branch—this makes it taste light and fresh.

Wheatgrass

Wheatgrass is a great source of vitamins and minerals, including B vitamins and the minerals calcium, phosphorus, sodium, potassium, magnesium, iron, and zinc.

- Wheatgrass contains all the essential amino acids in a form that is easily absorbed by the body.
- This grass can boost the immune system as it contains antioxidants.

Barley Grass

Slightly stronger in flavor than wheatgrass, barley grass is packed with antioxidants and acts as a free radical scavenger, protecting cells from damage.

- Known to reduce inflammation and pain, barley grass contains large amounts of minerals including calcium, magnesium, iron, phosphorus, zinc, B vitamins, vitamin E, folic acid, and protein.

Sprouted Seeds

During sprouting, minerals, such as calcium and magnesium, bind to protein making them more bioavailable. The quality of the protein and fiber content also improves when the seeds are sprouted.

- A very good source of antioxidants, sprouted seeds support cell regeneration, making them potent antiaging and rejuvenating foods.

Supergreen Mint and Cacao Ice Cream

ENERGIZING

This light refreshing ice cream is packed with supergreens for extra nutrition. Wheatgrass powder is fresh tasting and mild in flavor so ideal for adding to desserts and drinks. The addition of coconut gives this ice cream a delicious creamy texture.

Prep: 30 mins/Soak: 2 hrs

Ingredients (serves 6)

Scant 1 cup (125 g) cashews, soaked in water for 2 hours then drained
1 cup (250 ml) coconut water
2 teaspoons wheatgrass powder
1½ cups (60 g) dry unsweetened coconut
¼ cup (60 g) yacon syrup or coconut syrup
2 or 3 sprigs of mint
½ teaspoon peppermint extract, or to taste
Pinch of sea salt
Large handful of cacao nibs

Method

1 Put the drained nuts and coconut water into a blender and process until smooth. Add all the other ingredients, except the cacao nibs, and process until smooth.

2 Pour the mixture into an ice-cream machine and churn according to the manufacturer's directions. As the mixture begins to thicken add the cacao nibs and continue to churn until the ice cream is frozen. If you don't have an ice-cream machine, transfer the mixture to a freezerproof container, cover with a lid, and freeze for 3 to 4 hours, whisking to break up the ice crystals every hour until frozen.

3 Eat at once or freeze in a freezerproof container until required.

HIGH IN ANTIOXIDANTS	
Calories (per serving)	246
Protein	5.4 g
Total fat	18.5 g
of which saturated fat	8.6 g
Carbohydrates	24.7 g
of which sugars	12.3 g
Vitamins/minerals	K₁, B₆, iron, thiamin

Herbs, Superherbs, and Spices

Culinary herbs contain many nutrients as well as plenty of flavor to liven up a variety of raw dishes. If you are using dried herbs select organic brands and check that they have no added preservatives.

In addition to the popular culinary herbs, such as parsley, basil, sage, and cilantro, there are a variety of superherbs

Nutrition: Superherbs and spices are full of antioxidants, essential oils, vitamins, and phytosterols.
Benefits: Help the body to fight against germs and toxins, and also reduce inflammation.

or medicinal herbs that can be added to dishes and drinks to improve health and longevity, including maca and ashwagandha. These superherbs are extremely concentrated and potent so should be used infrequently in minute amounts—less than a teaspoon at a time.

There are also culinary spices that contain super properties, such as turmeric, which adds a vibrant yellow color to dishes and is a powerful anti-inflammatory.

Parsley

Parsley is an excellent source of vitamin C and beta-carotenes to help lower inflammation and support a healthy immune system.

- Parsley is rich in phytonutrients, including flavonoids and a number of volatile oils known for their anticancer properties.
- Parsley is a good source of folic acid, important for keeping the heart healthy.

Cilantro

Cilantro is rich in phytonutrients and volatile oils which are known for their antimicrobial benefits, making it helpful for treating stomach infections.

- Cilantro may aid in the removal of toxins, including heavy metals, from the body.
- This superherb may help to maintain healthy blood sugar levels.
- Cilantro contains iron to help anemia.

Mint

Mint contains volatile oils, such as menthol, known for their carminative effects on digestive health.

- Mint prevents the growth of harmful bacteria including *Helicobacter pylori*.
- Rich in the volatile oil rosmarinic acid known for its anti-inflammatory benefits, mint may ease respiratory conditions, such as asthma.

Basil

Rich in flavonoids and volatile oils, basil also has antibacterial properties.

- A good source of beta-carotene, basil helps keep the immune system healthy.
- Basil contains magnesium, which helps cardiovascular health and allows muscles and blood vessels to relax.
- Basil also contains vitamins K and C for healthy bones.

Pistachio Pesto

ANTIAGING

Give your normal pesto a makeover with this version using pistachios. You can increase the omega-3 content by using flaxseed or hemp seed oil instead of olive oil. The addition of nutritional yeast flakes provides a lovely "cheesy" flavor without the need for dairy. This is delicious tossed in zucchini noodles.

Prep: 5 mins

Ingredients (serves 6)

2 garlic cloves

Scant ½ cup (60 g) shelled pistachios

1¼ cups (30 g) basil leaves

1 tablespoon lemon juice

½ teaspoon sea salt

1 tablespoon nutritional yeast flakes

5 tablespoons extra-virgin olive oil, flaxseed oil, or hemp seed oil

Freshly ground black pepper

Method

1 Simply place all the ingredients in a food processor and process until the mixture is smooth.

2 Taste and adjust the seasoning if necessary then serve with zucchini and carrot noodles or over shredded vegetables. Store the pesto in the refrigerator for up to a week.

PROMOTES HEALTHY SKIN	
Calories (per serving)	183
Protein	3 g
Total fat	18.2 g
of which saturated fat	2.5 g
Carbohydrates	1.9 g
of which sugars	0.6 g
Vitamins/minerals	B, E, iron, magnesium

Sage

Sage has long been valued as both a culinary and medicinal herb.

- Sage contains a variety of volatile oils, flavonoids, and phenolic acids, including rosmarinic acid, which can help to improve memory.
- Sage contains high levels of antioxidants, to help soothe the digestive system when drunk as a tea.

Thyme

Aromatic, evergreen thyme has a long history of use for chest and respiratory problems including bronchitis.

- The volatile oil components of thyme have potent antimicrobial properties, making it helpful for soothing stomach infections.
- Rich in phytonutrients, thyme may help protect the body from aging.

Ashwagandha

Ashwagandha is a traditional adaptogenic superherb (as it enhances endurance), and is popular in many parts of India and Asia. Use as a powder or tea.

- Ashwagandha is used as an adaptogen rejuvenating tonic, sedative, and immune supporting food.
- Valued as an antiaging superherb, ashwagandha may calm the mind.

Aloe Vera

Aloe vera, known as "the plant of immortality" by the Egyptians, has been used medicinally for over 5,000 years. It is available as a juice.

- This superherb's healing properties are numerous, including being anti-inflammatory, cleansing, and having a positive effect on the immune system.
- Aloe is also useful in aiding digestion.

Maca

A favorite superherb in South America, maca is regarded as an all-round energy tonic. It is sometimes called "Peruvian ginseng." A member of the cruciferous family, its radishlike tuberous roots have numerous health benefits. Maca has a nutty, light flavor with a slight butterscotch edge. It is usually available as a powder.

- A known adaptogen, maca has the ability to help the body adjust to stress, build up resistance to disease, and support the immune system.
- Maca also appears to work directly on the hypothalamus and pituitary glands, which are the "master glands" of the body, whose role is to regulate the other glands. This makes maca very helpful for balancing sex hormone levels, bringing relief to menstrual symptoms, including premenstrual syndrome (PMS), and alleviating menopausal symptoms.

Ginseng

Ginseng is usually used as a general tonic and adaptogen to help the body resist the stresses placed upon it on a daily basis. Available as a powder or tincture.

- Superherb ginseng improves the immune system, reduces inflammation, improves insulin sensitivity, and helps with physical and mental performance, vitality, and reduces fatigue.

He Shou Wu

He shou wu is widely used in Chinese tonic herbalism to prevent premature aging by toning the kidneys and liver, nourishing the blood, and fortifying the muscles, tissues, and bones. Use as powder and tea.

- Superherb he shou wu is used to enhance sexual drive, increase sperm count, and strengthen the sperm and ova as it is rich in zinc and iron.

Gynostemma

An adaptogenic superherb, gynostemma is popularly used to invigorate the body and restore strength and vitality, as well as to calm the body to relieve anxiety. Available as a tea or powder.

- The main active ingredients in gynostemma are saponins, which are antioxidants. It aids the liver and binds with bile acids to reduce cholesterol.

Mucuna Pruriens

Superherb mucuna, also known as velvet bean, has long been used in Ayurvedic medicine to help with health and mood. Available as a powder or in capsule form.

- Mucuna is best known for containing a very powerful neurotransmitter precursor called L-dopa—an amino acid that converts into dopamine, making it effective for boosting mood.

Shilajit

Shilajit is an Ayurvedic superherb and a potent mineral supplement. It is a brown pitch or tar that exudes from layers of rocks in several mountain ranges of the world. It is used to mineralize the body and restore vigor. Available as a powder.

- Shilajit contains humic and fulvic acid known for their antiviral and detoxifying properties.

Turmeric

Turmeric is a culinary superspice that adds color and flavor to many Indian dishes.

- Turmeric's health benefits lie in its active ingredient, called curcumin, which is known for its potent anti-inflammatory and antioxidant properties. Research into its ability to aid autoimmune and inflammatory conditions is positive and may be valuable for Alzheimer's disease.

Mushrooms

Scientific and nutritional studies of numerous varieties of edible mushrooms show that many of these tasty fungi are excellent for your health. Button, cremini, and portobello mushrooms are all good marinated then dehydrated before adding to salads, soups, or wraps.

Mushrooms are not only nutritious but are known for their health-giving properties, especially for keeping the immune system healthy as well as improving energy, endurance, and vitality. They are also helpful for maintaining a healthy weight as well as improving vitamin D levels.

Mushrooms contain a range of health-giving compounds, such as mannose, known for its antimicrobial and antiviral action, which is especially useful for urinary tract infections. In addition to fresh mushrooms, certain mushrooms—often referred to as medicinal mushrooms—such as chaga, cordyceps, and reishi mushrooms (see page 99), are available dried, as a loose powder, tea, or extract. They are also sometimes available as part of a mixed powdered formula.

Always choose organically grown mushrooms because they absorb whatever they grow in and have the ability to concentrate toxins.

Health Benefits of Mushrooms

 Stress: Mushrooms provide a range of B vitamins that are important for supporting the adrenals. Certain mushrooms like reishi are also known adaptogens (as it enhances endurance), helping the body to counter daily stresses.

 Cardiovascular health: Mushrooms provide plenty of B vitamins, important for lowering elevated homocysteine, which is a risk factor for cardiovascular disease. High in antioxidants and fiber they can help maintain healthy levels of cholesterol.

 Anticancer: Certain mushrooms —including cordyceps, reishi, and shiitake—have been shown to have anticancer and antitumor benefits.

 Immune system: Mushrooms are rich in polysaccharides, which have a beneficial effect on the immune system. They also provide vitamin D that is important to keep the immune system healthy and possess antibacterial and antiviral properties.

 Healthy weight: A good source of protein and fiber, mushrooms are low in carbohydrates and are very helpful for maintaining a healthy weight.

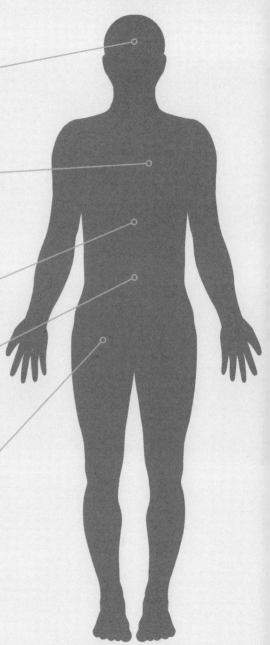

Shiitake Mushrooms

Shiitake mushrooms are native to East Asia and are available fresh and dried. Use them in dishes instead of button mushrooms.

- Shiitake mushrooms contain B vitamins to support memory and adrenal health.
- They are a good source of vitamin D for keeping bones strong.
- Shiitake mushrooms are packed with antioxidants to help the immune system.

Button Mushrooms

Button mushrooms are the white, young stage of the common cultivated variety.

- Button mushrooms contain copper, needed to produce blood cells.
- A good source of B vitamins for energy.
- Button mushrooms are rich in potassium, which can prevent heart attacks.
- These little mushrooms contain lots of iron to help prevent anemia.

Cremini Mushrooms

Cremini mushrooms are also known as brown cap or chestnut mushrooms.

- A good source of B vitamins to keep the cardiovascular system healthy.
- Cremini mushrooms supply conjugated linolenic acid (CLA), a healthy fat known for its anti-inflammatory properties.
- Rich in antioxidant nutrients, cremini can help to lower chronic inflammation.

Reishi Mushrooms

The reishi mushroom is also known as the "mushroom of immortality" and is considered by many to be a tonic because of its ability to boost the immune system and to promote longevity. Often available as powder or capsules.

- Reishi has adaptogenic properties (it enhances endurance), helping the body to calm worries and anxiety in daily life.

Chaga Mushrooms

Chaga is a popular medicinal mushroom and is used as a tonic. Available as powder.

- Chaga has strong immune-enhancing properties, with high levels of antioxidants. Its many active ingredients, including sterols and saponins, help support the immune system.
- Chaga contains antiviral properties to treat diseases, such as colds and flu.

Cordyceps Mushrooms

Cordyceps is a mushroom that can be used as a tonic, strengthening the health of the kidneys, and also promoting lung and vascular health. Available in various forms including powder or as an extract.

- Cordyceps can be helpful in keeping the heart healthy by increasing the flow of blood and helping to regulate blood pressure.

Maitake Mushrooms

Maitake mushrooms are native to the mountains of northeastern Japan.

- Best known for its ability to detoxify some carcinogens through the beta glucan polysaccharides it contains, which help natural cell growth.
- Maitake mushrooms are beneficial in protecting the liver and aiding digestion.
- They fight bacterial and viral infections.

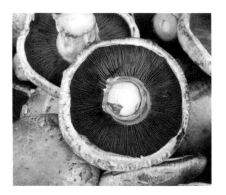

Portobello Mushrooms

Portobello belongs to the cremini family of mushrooms. With a distinctive earthy flavor, they are delicious marinated and dehydrated or used to replace burger buns.

- Rich in fiber and low in carbohydrates, portobello mushrooms are helpful in balancing blood sugar levels.
- Portobello's B vitamins, potassium, and phosphorous are good for bones.

Turkey Tail Mushrooms

Turkey tail mushrooms grow on dead trees, logs, and branches throughout the world, and get their name from their various colors, which look like a turkey tail. Available as a powder.

- Turkey tail mushrooms are high in antioxidants and help to strengthen the immune system, which in turn helps with respiratory ailments.

Mushroom Meatballs

HIGH FIBER

These delicious vegan "meatballs" are dehydrated to create a lovely crispy texture. Serve them with zucchini or carrot noodles or simply toss them into a mixed salad.

Prep: 45 mins/Dry: 2 hrs

Ingredients (makes 8, serves 2)

2½ oz (70 g) portobello mushrooms, chopped
½ cup (50 g) walnuts
2 tablespoons ground flaxseed
2 tablespoons nutritional yeast flakes
3 soft pitted dates
2 sundried tomatoes in oil, drained
1 tablespoon apple cider vinegar
1 teaspoon ground cumin
Handful of parsley
1 tablespoon tamari or coconut aminos
1 garlic clove
½ teaspoon sea salt
⅓ cup (30 g) ground almonds, for coating

Method

1 Place the mushrooms and walnuts in a food processor and blend until broken up. Add the remaining ingredients, except the ground almonds, and process to form a chunky paste. Chill for 30 minutes.

2 Take walnut-size balls of the mixture and dust in a little ground almonds.

3 Place the balls on a nonstick sheet and dehydrate at 115°F (46°C) for 2 hours, flipping them halfway through. Serve the meatballs with a fresh salad.

EXCELLENT FOR BOOSTING ENERGY	
Calories (per serving)	346
Protein	13 g
Total fat	26.8 g
of which saturated fat	2.9 g
Carbohydrates	14.7 g
of which sugars	6.7 g
Vitamins/minerals	B, magnesium, copper

Beans, Pulses, and Sprouted Seeds

Beans, pulses, or legumes, and certain seeds need to be soaked and sprouted before they can be eaten raw. Kidney beans, however, are one of the few beans that should never be eaten raw.

There are a wide variety of sprouted beans and pulses that can be incorporated into a raw food diet and many of them are good sources of protein. Sprouting not only increases digestibility but also greatly enhances the seed's nutritional profile.

Sprouting is essentially germinating the plant and thereby creating a "living food." This leads to a rapid increase in the vitamin content as well as making the protein, fats, carbohydrates, and minerals in the food easier to digest and be absorbed into the body, for example, the vitamin C content of seeds increases dramatically when sprouted. Sprouts are easy to grow at home, just make sure to buy organic seeds and ensure the sprouter or jar is clean.

Health Benefits of Beans, Pulses, and Sprouted Seeds

 Heart health: These foods are rich in B vitamins, magnesium, and potassium plus fiber—all essential nutrients for supporting a healthy heart, lowering high cholesterol, and maintaining a healthy blood pressure.

 Muscle mass: Many sprouted beans and seeds are a useful source of protein to support muscle mass. Vitamin C aids the production of collagen for connective tissue and also reduces oxidative stress to support quick recovery after exercise.

 Detoxification: High in fiber to aid excretion and support beneficial bacteria that is important for detoxification. Some sprouted beans support detoxification pathways and the elimination of toxins from the body.

 Blood sugar: Because they have a low glycemic index (GI), sprouted beans and pulses do not adversely affect blood sugar levels. Some, such as fenugreek, also appear to improve insulin function making them a useful addition to support healthy blood sugar levels for people with diabetes.

 Energy: A good source of copper, iron, and B vitamins as well as magnesium which help the conversion of carbohydrates to energy in the body. Being rich in protein and fiber they also help support healthy blood sugar levels so avoiding energy dips.

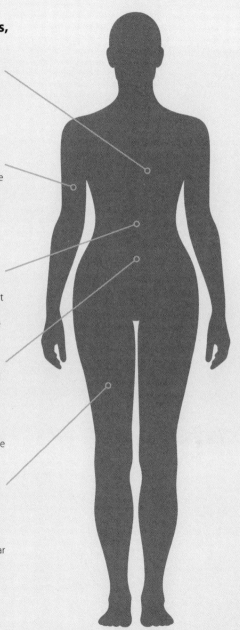

Sprouting

Before sprouting you need to soak the dry seeds or beans in water. While the soaking time varies depending on the bean or grain, for simplicity you can soak them overnight. Rinse and drain in the morning. Place in a sprouter or jam jar covered with a piece of cheesecloth or a mesh lid. Rinse and drain daily until they are ready to use.

Nutrition: Sprouts are incredibly nutritious and are packed with vitamins, minerals, and antioxidants. **Benefits:** High in fiber so a good aid to digestion, they can also help reduce cholesterol levels.

Depending on the type of seed or bean you use this can take from one to five days. The quantity of sprouts produced from dry seed varies but as a general rule one cup of dry seed or bean will yield around two to three cups of sprouts. Many of the following seeds can be bought ready sprouted from health food stores.

A few seeds—such as wheat, sunflower, pea, and buckwheat—require planting in shallow soil, after soaking, to sprout.

Alfalfa Sprouts

The alfalfa plant is related to the pea family. Rich in protein and vitamins A, C, and K, it is also packed with antioxidants and minerals including magnesium, calcium, and iron.

- Alfalfa are high in phytoestrogens, which can alleviate menopausal symptoms.
- Alfalfa contains high levels of amino acid called canavanine, which can aggravate inflammatory conditions.

Broccoli Sprouts

Broccoli sprouts are easy to grow and have a pleasant mild flavor and crunchy texture.
- These sprouts contain large amounts of glucoraphanin, a precursor to the compound sulforaphane, shown to protect cells from cancer-causing chemicals. Some studies suggest that the sprouts have ten to 20 times more sulforaphane than whole broccoli.

Fenugreek Sprouts

Traditionally, fenugreek is used for digestive problems and improves breast milk secretion in nursing mothers.
- Fenugreek sprouts may improve insulin secretion.
- The high fiber content in these sprouts helps stabilize blood sugar.
- A good source of iron and copper to support healthy red blood cells.

Lentil Sprouts

Lentils come in a variety of colors and different sizes and are an excellent source of protein and fiber.
- Lentil sprouts are rich in copper, which is important for healthy connective tissue and promoting adenosine triphosphate (ATP) energy production.
- Sprouted lentils are rich in zinc and vitamin C to boost the immune system.

Mung Bean Sprouts

Mung beans are rich in fiber and protein to support healthy blood sugar levels.

- The high fiber content of these bean sprouts helps with the growth of beneficial bacteria in the gut and the production of short chain fatty acids, which can protect against colon cancer.
- A good source of B vitamins and magnesium to keep the heart healthy.

Buckwheat Sprouts

Buckwheat is not a cereal grain but actually a fruit seed that is related to rhubarb.

- Buckwheat sprouts are gluten free and are particularly rich in the minerals manganese, magnesium, and copper to help boost energy.
- High in flavonoids, particularly rutin, they are shown to protect against cardiovascular disease.

Quinoa Sprouts

Quinoa is an ancient seed that can be soaked and sprouted for one to two days.

- High in fiber and protein, quinoa contains all the essential amino acids our bodies need.
- A good source of magnesium, potassium, zinc, and iron, sprouting helps reduce phytic acid making these essential minerals more bioavailable.

Buckwheat Cereal

GLUTEN FREE

This "cereal" is delicious as a raw snack or served with almond or other nut milk as a healthy breakfast option. Add cacao powder to create a luxurious chocolatey flavor. You can also sprinkle on some crunchy nuts and seeds or dried fruit, to make it even tastier.

Prep: 25 mins/Dry: 12 hrs

Ingredients (serves 4)

1 cup (170 g) buckwheat groats, soaked in cold water for 20 minutes and drained
4 tablespoons yacon syrup, maple syrup, or coconut syrup
2 tablespoons cacao powder, optional
Pinch of sea salt

Method

1 Combine all the ingredients in a medium bowl and stir until mixed.

2 Spread the mixture onto a nonstick sheet in an even layer.

3 Dehydrate at about 110°F (46°C) for 10 to 12 hours or overnight until dry. Break the dried granola into chunks and store in an airtight container. This will keep for at least a week.

4 To serve, place the buckwheat cereal in a bowl and pour over the nut milk of your choice.

GREAT FOR THE IMMUNE SYSTEM	
Calories (per serving)	231
Protein	4.7 g
Total fat	1.3 g
of which saturated fat	0.4 g
Carbohydrates	63.7 g
of which sugars	16.3 g
Vitamins/minerals B, iron, magnesium, zinc	

Fruits

Fruits are packed with antioxidants, vitamins, and minerals making them an excellent addition to a raw food diet.

While there is a temptation on a raw food diet to consume high quantities of fruit this is not recommended due to the high carbohydrate and fructose content. Fruit, however, are a rich source of vitamins, including vitamins C and A, minerals, antioxidants, and fiber so can reduce the risk of strokes, heart disease, maintain healthy blood pressure, and can protect against some cancers.

Dried fruits tend to be high in sugars and glycemic load (GL) so should be eaten in small amounts and their use when making raw desserts and cookies limited. For people with blood sugar imbalances or inflammatory conditions it is recommended to avoid all fruit juices, fruit smoothies, and dried fruit, and limit fruit to around two portions a day. This will keep the fructose intake low in the diet.

Citrus fruits and berries are typically lower in sugar than other fruits yet provide a wealth of health benefits, so if you are concerned about sugar content focus more on these lower fructose fruits. If you want to maximize your antioxidant benefits from fruits it is best to choose organic, seasonal produce. Frozen fruit is a very healthy alternative when the fruit is out of season.

Health Benefits of Fruits

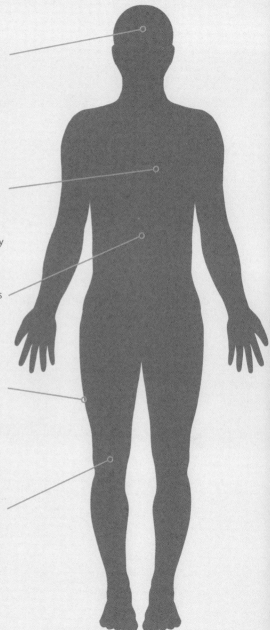

 Brain health: Many fruits provide B vitamins that may contribute to improved memory. Folate, present in most fruits, also contributes to the production of serotonin and can help with depression and to improve mood. Certain fruits, such as berries rich in anthocyanins, have been shown to reduce cognitive decline.

 Heart health: Fruits contain a lot of antioxidants, B vitamins, and fiber that offer a protective benefit for the heart, lower homocysteine, and reduce inflammation. Many fruits are rich in potassium to help maintain healthy blood pressure.

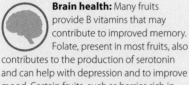 **Anticancer:** Fruits contain various phytochemicals known for their cancer-fighting properties, such as ellagic acid and limonene. High in fiber, they also support the excretion of harmful toxins and potential carcinogens.

 Skin health: Packed with water to hydrate the skin, fruits also supply plenty of vitamin C, which helps your body produce collagen to keep your skin firm and plump. They are also rich in antioxidants including carotenoids, which can help protect the skin from damage including UV damage.

 Bone health: Fruits are packed with antioxidants to lower inflammation associated with arthritis plus vitamin C for the production of collagen, which is important for connective tissue and bone health.

Berries and Cherries

Berries and cherries are powerful fruits to enhance your health. They contain antioxidants to help protect the body from the harmful effects of free radicals as well as lowering the risk of heart disease and improving blood sugar levels. They are excellent for keeping the brain healthy and to help support memory in older people.

Nutrition: Berries and cherries contain high amounts of antioxidants, including flavonoids.
Benefits: They can keep you mentally sharp, reduce the risk of heart attacks, and lower blood pressure.

Raspberry

Not only are raspberries delicious, they are a good source of fiber that aids digestion and balances blood sugar levels.

- Low in sugar, raspberries are rich in polyphenols such as anthocyanin, flavonols, and ellagic acid that have cancer-fighting properties.
- Raspberries contain lots of vitamin C to support a healthy immune system.

Blackberry

Blackberries are low in calories, virtually fat free, and high in fiber—ideal for anyone trying to maintain or lose weight.

- Blackberries are particularly rich in antioxidants, including bioflavonoids and vitamin C, and may help protect against cognitive decline.
- Their high tannin content can alleviate diarrhea and reduce inflammation.

Blueberry

Packed with phytochemicals including anthocyanins together with vitamin C, vitamin E, and carotenoids, blueberries help boost the immune system.

- The high content of anthocyanins in blueberries, which gives them their blue color, reduces the risk of heart disease.
- Blueberries are high in fiber so help prevent constipation.

Strawberry

One of the most popular berries, choose strawberries that are firm, plump, and deep red to get the most of their nutrients.

- An excellent source of vitamin C and polyphenol antioxidants, strawberries boost the immune system and keep the skin and eyes healthy.
- Being rich in antioxidants, strawberries protect against cardiovascular disease.

Cherry

Sweet or sour, cherries are packed full of health-promoting nutrients.

- Sweet cherries are rich in vitamin C, carotenoids, and anthocyanins, which protect against certain cancers.
- Tart cherries contain melatonin to help with sleep difficulties.
- Cherries are anti-inflammatory and can help to reduce arthritic pain.

Berry Cheesecake

ENERGIZING

This delicious raw vegan dessert is packed with healthy fats and protein to keep you energized. This dish is great for freezing and can be served as a fantastic iced dessert, too. Simply remove from the freezer 30 minutes before you wish to serve.

Prep: 45 mins/Chill: 3 to 4 hrs

Ingredients (serves 10)
Base
1 cup (150 g) cashews
1 cup (90 g) dry unsweetened coconut, plus extra to decorate
Pinch of sea salt
Juice and grated zest of 1 lemon
2 tablespoons coconut oil, melted

Filling
1⅔ cups (250 g) cashews
⅓ cup (60 g) xylitol
2 teaspoons vanilla extract
½ cup (100 g) coconut oil, melted

1½ cups (225 g) fresh berries of choice e.g. blackberries, blueberries, raspberries, plus extra to serve
Scant ½ cup (100 ml) pomegranate juice
Juice of ½ lemon

Method

1 Make the base by grinding the nuts and coconut in a blender until fine. Stir in the remaining base ingredients to form a sticky dough and press firmly into the bottom of an 8-in (20-cm) springform cake pan. Place in the freezer for 30 minutes to harden.

2 Place all the filling ingredients into a blender or food processor and process until smooth. Pour the mixture over the base and chill for 3 to 4 hours until set. You can freeze it at this point until required.

3 Remove the cheesecake from the pan and top with berries and a little dry unsweetened coconut to serve.

HELPS TO STABILIZE BLOOD SUGAR LEVELS	
Calories (per serving)	425
Protein	7.9 g
Total fat	37.9 g
of which saturated fat	19.9 g
Carbohydrates	15.4 g
of which sugars	4.5 g
Vitamins/minerals	C, B₆, K₁, copper, zinc

Citrus Fruit

Citrus fruits are low fructose fruits packed with beneficial antioxidants and essential nutrients that keep the heart healthy and reduce the risk of some chronic diseases. Adding lemon or lime to green juices and smoothies can provide plenty of vitamin C. A good source of fiber, citrus can also be useful in helping weight loss.

Nutrition: Citrus fruits are high in vitamin C, good sources of folate and thiamin, and contain flavonoids.

Benefits: Help to boost the immune system and may help to protect against cancer and heart disease.

Lemon

Having a drink of warm lemon juice early in the morning helps to flush out toxins, alkalize the body, and aid digestion.

- Lemons are hydrating, so are ideal for cleansing and rejuvenating the skin.
- Lemons are also a good source of pectin fiber, to help with the elimination of toxins from the body and relieve constipation and indigestion.

Lime

Packed with vitamin C, limes also contain anticancer limonoid phytochemicals.

- Limes are rich in citric acid, which is a natural inhibitor of kidney stones made of crystallized calcium.
- The primary flavonoid found in limes, known as hesperidin, has been shown to lower cholesterol and triglyceride levels, making them ideal for a healthy heart.

Orange

Oranges contain plenty of vitamin C and phytochemicals, providing antioxidant protection and a boost to the immune system to help it function well.

- Rich in flavonoids, oranges help with cardiovascular health and possess cancer-protective properties.
- Oranges are high in fiber.
- They contain calcium and potassium.

Grapefruit

Known for their ability to support weight loss, grapefruits are packed with fiber and water, which helps you feel fuller for longer and supports healthy blood sugar levels.

- Naringenin, a phytochemical found in grapefruit, is known to successfully prevent the formation of kidney cysts, and also protects the body from developing cancer.

Tangerine

Tangerines are a specific variant of mandarin oranges, which are reddish orange in color.

- Low in calories, tangerines contain lots of vitamin C, folate, and beta-carotene.
- Tangerines are a good source of potassium, which is necessary for the health of the kidneys, muscles, nerves, heart, and digestive system.

Orange Mango Nut Yogurt

HIGH FIBER

A simple deliciously creamy dessert which also makes an ideal breakfast option or snack, serve this with some fruit or top with a sprinkling of nuts and seeds. You can also ferment this nut yogurt by adding a spoonful of probiotic powder and letting it stand overnight at room temperature. The next day, put into the refrigerator until needed.

Prep: 5 mins

Ingredients (serves 4)

⅔ cup (100 g) almonds
Generous ¾ cup (200 ml) fresh orange juice
½ mango, chopped
3 tablespoons lucuma powder
1 teaspoon vanilla extract
Orange segments, to decorate

Method

1 Place all the ingredients in a blender and process until smooth, adding a little more orange juice if the mixture is too thick.

2 Store in the refrigerator until needed. Spoon the yogurt into individual glasses and decorate with orange segments before serving.

PROMOTES A HEALTHY HEART	
Calories (per serving)	233
Protein	6.5 g
Total fat	14.1 g
of which saturated fat	1.1 g
Carbohydrates	19.4 g
of which sugars	8.7 g
Vitamins/minerals	C, E, B, magnesium

Tropical Fruit

Tropical fruits are a popular choice for using in both sweet and savory dishes as well as green smoothies and frozen desserts. They contain lots of nutrients and phytochemicals and are rich in antioxidants such as carotenes, vitamin C, and flavonoids to promote health. They also have potent anti-inflammatory properties.

Nutrition: Tropical fruit are nutritious as they are full of vitamins, minerals, essential nutrients, and flavor.

Benefits: Protect the heart, lower cholesterol, reduce inflammation, and look after the kidneys.

Papaya

Packed with vitamin C and carotenoids, papaya are a good choice for keeping the immune system and eyes healthy.

- Papaya contains several protein-digesting enzymes including papain. These enzymes have been shown to help lower inflammation, making them ideal for treating arthritis and supporting recovery after exercise.

Mango

Mangoes are an excellent source of fiber to aid digestion and lower cholesterol.

- Rich in vitamins C and A and antioxidants including quercetin, mangoes help reduce inflammation and protect the body from certain cancers.
- Mangoes are a very good source of iron, which is helpful for people with anemia.

Pineapple

Pineapples are abundant in vitamin C and bromelain, a digestive enzyme known to lower inflammation that is helpful for joint disorders and respiratory conditions.

- Pineapples are a good source of fiber, important for a healthy digestive system.
- Rich in manganese, pineapples can help to strengthen bones and connective tissues, as well as boost energy.

Banana

A very popular fruit, bananas are rich in pectin which helps with digestion— relieving constipation and diarrhea.

- Bananas are a good source of potassium, helpful for relieving muscle cramps.
- Bananas contain B_6 and tryptophan to help boost mood by supporting the production of serotonin, our mood boosting neurotransmitter.

Lychee

Lychees are an excellent source of vitamin C for keeping the immune system healthy.

- These fruits are high in fiber to balance blood sugar levels.
- Lychees contain vitamin C, B vitamins, especially B_6, and potassium, which helps control blood pressure.
- A good source of copper for healthy bones and connective tissue.

Tropical Green Smoothie

HYDRATING

A delicious creamy blend, this is the perfect smoothie to kick-start the day. Freezing the banana before blending creates a wonderful thick, creamy texture. Add a scoop of vegan protein powder to boost the protein content. This is also an easy way to sneak more greens into your diet and boost nutrition with superfood powders.

Prep: 10 mins

Ingredients (serves 1)

3½ oz (100 g) fresh mango, chopped
½ banana, chopped and frozen
1 large handful of spinach leaves
1 teaspoon wheatgrass powder
1 cup (250 ml) coconut water or water
4 ice cubes

Method

1 Place all the ingredients, except the ice, into a blender and process until the mixture is smooth and creamy.

2 Add the ice and blend briefly to combine, then pour into a glass and serve immediately.

CLEANSING AND ALKALIZING	
Calories (per serving)	233
Protein	6.5 g
Total fat	14.1 g
of which saturated fat	1.1 g
Carbohydrates	19.4 g
of which sugars	8.7 g
Vitamins/minerals	A, C, K₁, potassium

Dragon Fruit

Also known as pitaya, dragon fruit is rich in vitamins C, B_1, B_2, and B_3, and minerals such as iron, calcium, and phosphorus.

- Dragon fruit contains antioxidants to protect cells from damage.
- A good source of fiber, dragon fruit can help to balance blood sugar levels.
- These fruits contain monounsaturated fats to keep the heart healthy.

Durian

Unlike most other fruits durian is high in fats and calories. It is sometimes called the "king of fruits" in Southeast Asia.

- As durian is high in carbohydrates and potassium it can quickly replenish energy levels and balance electrolytes.
- Durian are a good source of vitamin C and B vitamins to help support the nervous and immune systems.

Kiwi

Loaded with more vitamin C than an equivalent amount of orange, kiwi can help to support the immune system and protect against inflammatory conditions such as asthma.

- Kiwis are high in fiber to help lower cholesterol and aid in digestion.
- A good source of vitamin K, kiwis are important for keeping bones healthy.

Longan Berry

Native to China, this yellow brown berry has a leathery protective shell and is closely related to the lychee. It is sometimes called "dragons eye" due to the white mark on the pit that looks like a pupil.

- Longan berries are a great source of vitamins A and C.
- They are rich in antioxidants and protect against chronic inflammation.

Date

Rich in dietary fiber, dates are very useful for relieving constipation and aiding the excretion of cholesterol from the body.

- Dates contain large amounts of iron and B vitamins to boost energy.
- A good source of potassium, dates help to regulate blood pressure and promote a healthy nervous system.
- Dates contain vitamin K for bone health.

Fig

Available fresh and dried, figs are high in natural sugars that can add sweetness to a variety of raw dishes.

- Figs are high in fiber, which helps to relieve constipation.
- They are a good source of vitamin B_6, which is important for the production of neurotransmitters, including serotonin, to boost mood.

Mangosteen

Low in calories and high in fiber, purple mangosteens are packed with a wealth of vitamins and minerals including potassium, manganese, magnesium, B vitamins, and vitamin C.

- Mangosteens are rich in phytochemicals including xanthones—powerful antioxidants that may have properties that help to protect against cancer.

Loquat

Loquats are a good source of vitamins A and C, to keep the skin and eyes healthy.

- Loquats provide copper, iron, and B vitamins to help with red blood cell formation and boost energy levels.
- Loquats are rich in pectin, a fiber useful for lowering cholesterol, removing toxins from the body, and also helping to reduce the risk of colon cancer.

Kumquat

Kumquats are small tropical citrus fruits that are eaten whole including the skin.

- Kumquats contain antioxidants like vitamins A, C, E, as well as phytonutrients that protect the body from harmful free radicals, making it useful for keeping the heart healthy.
- A rich source of calcium, kumquats can help to strengthen the bones.

Pomegranate

Pomegranates come from the Middle East and have been used medicinally for years.

■ Pomegranates are rich in vitamin C and help to boost the immune system.

■ Pomegranates contain antioxidants to help reduce joint pain and decrease inflammation in arthritic conditions.

■ Pomegranates are a good source of B vitamins, vitamin K, and potassium.

Cantaloupe Melon

The orange flesh of the cantaloupe is packed with beta-carotene which converts to vitamin A in the body and helps to protect the skin and eyes from UV damage.

■ Cantaloupe melons are rich in vitamin C needed for the production of collagen.

■ These melons provide plenty of potassium, which is important to keep a healthy fluid balance in the body.

Watermelon

Hydrating and rich in antioxidants and vitamins A and C, watermelon is perfect for promoting healthy skin.

■ The amino acid L-citrulline in watermelon relieves muscle soreness and improves recovery after exercise.

■ Watermelon is a good source of lycopene, which protects against prostate cancer.

Raw Fig Bars

ALKALIZING

This delicious sweet cake bar is high in fiber and protein to keep you feeling energized throughout the day. These bars will keep for up to one week in the refrigerator or can be frozen for up to one month.

Prep: 20 mins/Freeze: 30 mins

Ingredients (makes 16 slices)

5 oz (150 g) dried figs

Crumbly crust layer

1⅔ cups (250 g) almonds
Generous ¾ cup (125 g) pecans
¼ cup (25 g) dry unsweetened coconut
⅓ cup (50 g) ground flaxseed
5 oz (150 g) dried dates
1 tablespoon orange juice
1 teaspoon ground cinnamon

Method

1 Place the figs in a bowl of warm water and let soak for 15 minutes. Drain them and process in a food processor to form a smooth thick paste. Set aside.

2 To make the base and topping, place the nuts, coconut, and ground flaxseed in a food processor and process to form crumbs. Add the dates, orange juice, and cinnamon and process until the mixture is combined. If it is too dry add a little more orange juice.

3 Line an 8-in (20-cm) square baking pan with plastic wrap. Press two-thirds of the mixture into the baking pan and spread the fig puree evenly on top. Crumble the remaining mixture over the puree and press it gently into the fig filling.

4 Place the baking pan in the freezer for 30 minutes to harden. Carefully remove the fig crumble and cut into bars. Store in the refrigerator or freeze until required.

HIGH IN FIBER AND MINERALS	
Calories (per slice)	223
Protein	5.3 g
Total fat	16.6 g
of which saturated fat	2.1 g
Carbohydrates	13 g
of which sugars	12 g
Vitamins/minerals	E, B, K, potassium

Orchard Fruit

Don't overlook the health benefits of everyday fruits like apples, pears, and plums, as these fruits are also a good source of vitamins and minerals and play an important role in preventing vitamin deficiencies, especially in vitamins A and C. Eat a variety of different types and colors of fruit to give the body the mix of nutrients

Nutrition: Orchard fruit are naturally low in fat, calories, and sodium, and high in fiber, vitamin C, and folate. **Benefits:** Maintain healthy blood pressure, help reduce cholesterol levels, and help heal wounds quickly.

it needs. As many of these popular fruits are highly contaminated with pesticides, always buy organic produce.

Rich in fiber, these fruits are particularly useful for maintaining healthy cholesterol levels and also provide a range of antioxidants, vitamins, and minerals to lower blood pressure, reduce the risk of heart disease and stroke, help the immune system to function properly, keep the eyes healthy, and lower inflammation.

Pear

Pears provide an excellent source of fiber, including pectin, making them ideal for relieving constipation.

- Pears contain high levels of boron which helps the body to retain calcium to help keep bones strong.
- A low allergen fruit, pears provide vitamins C and E and potassium to keep blood pressure levels healthy.

Apple

A good source of pectin, a type of soluble fiber, apples are very useful in aiding the digestive system, as well as lowering total and LDL cholesterol.

- The flavonoids present in apples help protect against cardiovascular disease.
- Apples are rich in B vitamins to support metabolism, keep the nervous system healthy, and boost energy levels.

Peach

Peaches are low in calories and contain plenty of vitamins, including carotenoids that are helpful in maintaining optimal vision and vitamin C for healthy skin.

- Peaches provide a range of B vitamins that are important for cognitive function.
- A good source of zinc, which has antiaging properties and helps to maintain a healthy immune system.

Plum

Plums are rich in potassium, a mineral that helps to reduce the risk of strokes.

- Prunes or dried plums are packed with phytochemicals including anthocyanins which can protect the body from free radical damage.
- Especially rich in fiber, plums can help to relieve constipation.
- Plums contain vitamin K for bone health.

Apricot

Low in calories and high in fiber, apricots are rich in vitamin A to boost eye health.

- Apricots provide a significant source of potassium that helps to maintain proper fluid balance, aids in the proper functioning of muscle, helps regulate the heart rate, and lowers blood pressure by relaxing the tension of the blood vessel walls and arteries.

Nectarine

Similar to peaches, nectarines are rich in beta-carotene and vitamin C to keep skin healthy and youthful.

- A good source of the antioxidant lutein to support healthy eyes and reduce the risk of macular degeneration.
- Nectarines contain a number of essential minerals including calcium, magnesium, and potassium.

Grape

Grapes are one of the most popular fruits and contain a number of essential nutrients needed for an active and healthy life.

- Grapes are rich in phytonutrients, including resveratrol known for its antiaging properties.
- The wealth of antioxidants present in grapes make them protective against cardiovascular disease.

Green Appleade

CLEANSING

The addition of the apple and lemon cuts through the slightly bitter taste of the greens in this deliciously refreshing drink. You can also juice different greens, such as lettuce, watercress, or even kale.

Prep: 5 mins

Ingredients (serves 1)

½ cucumber

1 celery stick

1 lemon, peeled

1 apple, unpeeled

1 small handful of fresh mint leaves

2 handfuls of spinach

¼ cup (60 ml) fizzy water

Method

1 Put all the ingredients, except the water, through an electric juicer. Pour in the fizzy water and serve at once over ice cubes, if liked.

HELPS WITH HYDRATION	
Calories (per serving)	73
Protein	3.6 g
Total fat	0.9 g
of which saturated fat	0.1 g
Carbohydrates	12.1 g
of which sugars	12.0 g
Vitamins/minerals	A, C, K₁, folate

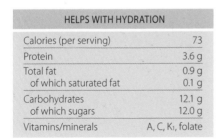

Superfruit

In addition to everyday fruits there are lots of "superfruits," which are exceptionally rich in antioxidants, fiber, vitamins, minerals, and other nutrients in a highly concentrated form. Each superfruit has their own unique set of health-promoting qualities. Many of these fruits are sold in powder or dried form making them useful pantry items for use all year round.

Nutrition: Superfruits are packed with antioxidants and anti-inflammatory nutrients that nourish your body.
Benefits: Boost the immune system, have antiaging effects, help keep the skin healthy, and aid digestion.

Add the powders to drinks or raw food dishes or eat the dried fruits as a snack.

Acai Berry

The acai berry is dark purple and similar in size to a blueberry. It is the fruit of a palm tree that grows in the Amazon rainforests—often called "the tree of life." Available as a freeze-dried powder and unsweetened frozen pulp.

- Acai berries are incredibly rich in antioxidants, particularly anthocyanins.
- High in vitamins C and A, and calcium.

Amla Berry

Also known as Indian gooseberry, the amla berry is a rich source of vitamin C, amino acids, polyphenols, lipids, and other essential oils. Available as a powder or in capsules.

- Amla berries are traditionally used to make an Indian jam, called chyavanprash, that helps to energize the body and give the immune system a healthy boost.

Baobab Fruit

Dried baobab powder is a fruit extract, made from the fruit of the baobab tree. Choose organic powder from sustainable and ethical baobab suppliers.

- Baobab fruit is high in vitamin C to help boost the immune system.
- Baobab is an alkalizing fruit, making it an energizing drink when mixed with water. It has a slightly tart, citrusy flavor.

Camu Camu Berry

These berries grow on a small bush native to the swampy lowlands of Peru. Available as a freeze-dried powder, it is used in small amounts, ¼ and ½ teaspoon daily—an excess may have a laxative effect.

- Camu camu berries are high in vitamin C to reduce inflammation.
- These berries also contain B vitamins to help improve blood circulation.

Goji Berry

Also called wolfberries, goji berries are a very popular protein rich superfood.

- Goji berries are a good source of antioxidants, especially beta-carotene and zeaxanthin, making them useful in keeping the skin and eyes healthy.
- They contain a number of minerals including zinc, iron, copper, calcium, selenium, and phosphorus.

Inca Berry

Inca berries, also called golden berries or cape gooseberries, grow at high altitudes in the tropical regions of South America. The harvested berries are sundried, enhancing their citruslike flavor.

- Inca berries are rich in bioflavonoids and vitamins A and C, which help to lower inflammation and keep the immune system healthy.

Lucuma Fruit

The delicious Peruvian lucuma fruit is prepared as a powder and sold as a natural sweetener. It has a wonderful maple syrup flavor, adding a fabulous sweetness to drinks and desserts.

- Lucuma contains a variety of nutrients, including B vitamins, fiber, and minerals such as iron, potassium, calcium, and also phosphorous.

Macqui Berry

Macqui berries are from Chile and are known for their exceptionally high antioxidant levels and vitamin C.

- They are a wonderful antiaging fruit, helping to protect the body from cell-damaging free radicals. With powerful anti-inflammatory properties, the berry is useful for combating chronic diseases. Available as a powder.

Mulberry

An excellent source of vitamin C, mulberries are also high in protein, making them a useful energizing food.

- Sundried mulberries are renowned for their high antioxidant levels, including phytochemicals called anthocyanins, known for their anti- inflammatory, antimicrobial, and anticancer properties.
- They are an excellent source of iron.

Noni Fruit

Noni is the common name for *Morinda citrifolia*, a tropical tree native to Polynesia, especially Tahiti and Hawaii. The noni fruit and powder have a strong citrus flavor.

- Noni is a powerful immune-supporting fruit that is rich in antioxidants, including selenium, and phytochemicals, such as limonene—known for their anticancer properties.

Superfruit Truffles

HIGH ENERGY

These little chocolate bites are packed with superfruits to energize the body. A delicious chocolate candy—you can vary the dried fruit and powders according to taste. These truffles will keep in the refrigerator for a week or can be frozen for up to a month.

Prep: 20 mins/Soak: 30 mins
Chill: 2 hrs

Ingredients (makes 16 balls)
½ cup (115 g) cashew nut butter
¼ cup (60 g) yacon syrup
2 tablespoons cacao powder, plus extra
   for dusting
¼ cup (60 g) melted cacao butter
¼ cup (30 g) goji berries soaked in water
   for 30 minutes then drained
1 teaspoon baobab powder
Pinch of sea salt
1 teaspoon vanilla extract
1 teaspoon goji berry powder
¼ cup (30 g) shelled hemp seeds
¼ cup (30 g) dried mulberries or
   Inca berries

Method

1 Place the nut butter, syrup, cacao powder, and melted cacao butter in a food processor and process to combine. Add the remaining ingredients and process to form a sticky dough. Chill in the refrigerator for about 2 hours, or until firm. Alternatively, place in the freezer until firm.

2 When the mixture is firm use a spoon to scoop out walnut-size balls. Using clean hands, roll into balls and coat in cacao powder. Store in the refrigerator.

HELPS TO BOOST THE IMMUNE SYSTEM	
Calories (per slice)	101
Protein	2.6 g
Total fat	6.7 g
of which saturated fat	1.9 g
Carbohydrates	11.1 g
of which sugars	6.1 g
Vitamins/minerals	C, A, iron, potassium

Nuts and Seeds

Nuts and seeds are particularly beneficial for a raw food diet as they are extremely high in life sustaining nutrients including protein, healthy fats, minerals, and fiber, and help in disease prevention.

Keep a selection of nuts and seeds in your pantry, which can be blended into healthy "milk," smoothies, ground into flour, made into nut butters and raw sauces, sprinkled on top of salads, added to wraps, or eaten as healthy snacks.

Nuts and seeds contain nutritional inhibitors and toxic substances, which can be minimized or eliminated by soaking. These inhibitors and toxic substances are enzyme inhibitors, phytates (phytic acid), polyphenols (tannins), and goitrogens.

Soaking starts the germination process, which makes nuts and seeds more nutritious. Soaking nuts and seeds in warm water also neutralizes enzyme inhibitors present and encourages the production of numerous beneficial enzymes. The action of these enzymes also increases the absorption and bioavailability of certain vitamins, especially B vitamins. One of the easiest ways to do this is to soak them in a bowl of water overnight. The next day, drain and rinse before using.

Health Benefits of Nuts and Seeds

 Brain health: They are a good source of essential fats for brain health plus vitamin E to protect brain cells from oxidative stress. Nuts and seeds also provide B vitamins including folate, which improves neural health and reduces the risk of cognitive decline.

 Heart health: Nuts and seeds help reduce the risk of cardiovascular disease. They are high in fiber to reduce LDL cholesterol and contain a good dose of heart-healthy monounsaturated fats. Nuts are also rich in arginine, an amino acid that converts to nitric oxide in the body and helps blood vessels to relax.

 Immune system: Many nuts and seeds are rich in vitamin E, zinc, and selenium, which are all key nutrients to support a healthy immune system. They also contain protein important for production of white blood cells and healthy fats to lower inflammation.

 Healthy weight: Despite being rich in calories, studies have shown that consuming nuts and seeds can promote healthy weight loss. They are satisfying—a high satiety food—that is metabolized slowly by the body, due to their fat, protein, and fiber content.

 Skin health: Nuts are rich in healthy fats that nourish the skin and full of skin-friendly antioxidants like vitamin E. They have been shown to protect the skin from damage and improve the skin's circulation, yielding a healthier glow.

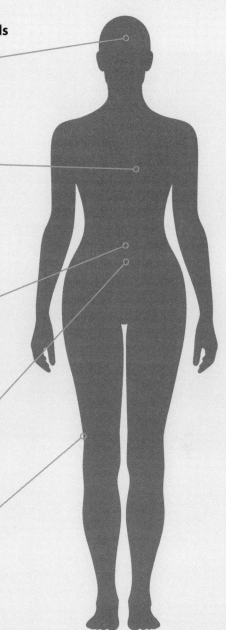

Nuts

Nuts are an excellent source of energy, antioxidants, vitamins, minerals and essential omega-3 fatty acids. Nuts contain fiber, which can help to lower cholesterol and make you feel fuller for longer. Nuts also contain L-arginine, a substance that can help to make artery walls more flexible and less prone to blockages.

Nutrition: Nuts are packed with protein, vitamins, minerals, essential fats, and fiber.
Benefits: Help to lower cholesterol levels, protect against heart disease, and may reduce the risk of strokes.

Macadamia

Macadamia nuts are rich in flavonoids known for their protective properties.

- Macadamia are high in palmitoleic acid and omega-7 fatty acids that promote fat burning and control appetite, making them helpful for weight management.
- These nuts are rich in bone supporting nutrients such as phosphorous, calcium, and manganese.

Pecan

Pecans are rich in vitamin E, an antioxidant to protect against heart disease.

- Pecans contain ellagic acid known for its anticancer properties.
- Rich in manganese, thiamin, magnesium, and copper, pecans are ideal for energy.
- Pecans contain zinc, which is good for keeping hair and skin healthy.

Walnut

Walnuts are a good source of protein and fiber, so will keep you feeling full for longer.

- One-quarter cup of walnuts provides more than the daily recommended value of plant-based omega-3 fatty acids, antioxidants, and the minerals copper, manganese, and molybdenum.
- Walnuts are rich in the amino acid L-arginine, for vascular health.

Almond

Almonds with skins on are the most nutritionally dense of all nuts.

- Almonds (particularly with the skin on) are rich in protective antioxidants including phenols and flavonoids, vitamin E, and potassium known for their heart healthy benefits.
- Almonds contain magnesium, calcium, and manganese to strengthen bones.

Cashew

Cashews are rich in a variety of minerals including iron, magnesium, and zinc, as well as protein.

- Cashews are rich in protective flavonols that may help reduce the risk of developing certain cancers.
- A good source of oleic acid, a healthy fat to help lower inflammation and promote a healthy heart.

Brazil Nut

Known for their high selenium content, Brazil nuts offer antioxidant protection, support the immune system, help wounds to heal, keep the heart healthy, and also help to maintain a healthy thyroid.

- Brazil nuts are also a good source of magnesium, phosphorus, and thiamin.
- These nuts are very high in protein and dietary fiber.

Why Eat Raw Cacao?

Cacao has been prized by many cultures for its health-giving properties as well as its delicious flavor. Raw, unsweetened cacao powder is very high in antioxidant flavonols to promote healthy aging. Particularly rich in iron, chromium, manganese, zinc, and copper, it is one of the richest food sources of magnesium, which helps to build strong teeth, relax the muscles, relieve stress, and relax the heart. Raw cacao also contains the amino acid tryptophan, which enhances relaxation and promotes better sleep, and phenylethylamine (PEA), which has a positive effect on mood.

Cacao nibs are made from cracking the dried bean. They are slightly bitter, have a strong chocolate flavor, and are delicious added to raw cookies, ice creams, and smoothies.

Cacao butter is derived from cold pressing cacao nibs to release the oil. Stir into smoothies, protein drinks, or use to make raw chocolate and cakes.

Raw cacao liquor is ground up raw beans that would normally be separated into raw cacao powder and butter. Delicious grated into dishes.

Seeds

Small, but packed with an array of nutrients, seeds are a healthy addition to a raw food diet. In fact, the only way to derive nutrition from seeds is to eat them raw as heating them destroys their nutrients. They provide a valuable source of protein and have a healthier ratio of omega-3 to -6 fatty acids than most nuts.

Nutrition: Seeds are packed with fiber, vitamins, and minerals including zinc, iron, calcium, and phosphorus. **Benefits:** Strengthen bones, help keep the immune system healthy, and promote healthy skin and hair.

Chia Seed

Chia seeds are prized for their high omega-3 content, which is important for brain health, lowering inflammation, and cardiovascular health.

- Very high in soluble fiber, chia seeds absorb water readily, making them good for digestive health, easing constipation, and creating a feeling of fullness. This makes them helpful when losing weight.

Flaxseed

Useful for stabilizing blood sugar level, flaxseeds can help to control appetite and aid weight loss. They are best eaten when ground.

- Flaxseed is a great source of essential omega-3, -6, and -9 fatty acids.
- Rich in lignans, which have fiberlike benefits, flaxseeds can help balance hormone levels.

Hemp Seed

Hemp seed is available as shelled seeds, whole seeds, and hemp oil. Its oil is an excellent source of essential omega-3 and -6 fatty acids in a balanced ratio for health.

- Hemp seeds are a good source of protein, containing all of the essential amino acids.
- They also contain B vitamins, vitamin E, antioxidants, and magnesium.

Sesame Seed

Sesame seeds are a great source of fiber. They are also rich in calcium, copper, and zinc, important for keeping bones healthy.

- A rich source of B vitamins, sesame seeds can help to improve memory and alleviate stress.
- Sesame seeds contain protein to help in the maintenance and development of muscles.

Sunflower Seed

Sunflower seeds are rich in vitamin E to protect the cells from oxidative damage and help keep the heart healthy.

- Sunflower seeds are a good source of thiamin, which assists in the conversion of carbohydrates into glucose.
- Sunflower seeds contain copper, important for producing melanin responsible for hair color.

Pumpkin Seed

Pumpkin seeds contain lots of minerals such as iron, magnesium, zinc, and copper.

- Known for their beneficial effects on the health of the prostate, pumpkin seed extracts and oils may play a role in treating an enlarged prostate.
- Pumpkin seeds contain tryptophan, an amino acid that the body converts into serotonin to boost mood.

Sacha Inchi

These jungle seeds from the Amazon rainforest of Peru are the size of a nut and have a wonderful rich taste.

- Sacha inchi are a good source of protein and fiber, making them ideal for maintaining a healthy weight.
- Exceptionally rich in omega-3 fatty acids, antioxidants, and vitamin E, sacha inchi help to keep the skin and hair healthy.

Pine Nut

Pine nuts are the seed from the pine cone and have a very delicate taste.

- Pine nuts are rich in pinolenic acid, which stimulates the secretion of a hormone produced by the intestines known as CCK that helps you feel full.
- An excellent source of fiber, pine nuts also provide vitamins E, K, and niacin.

Raw Chocolate Cookies

ENERGIZING

These crunchy cookies are rich in protein and fiber and make a deliciously sweet treat. You can add a selection of raw superfoods to this mixture to further boost the nutritional content, if desired.

Prep: 15 mins/Dry: 12 hrs

Ingredients
(makes around 16 cookies)

Generous ¾ cup (125 g) almonds

Scant 1¼ cups (180 g) cashews

5 oz (150 g) dried soft pitted dates

2 tablespoons coconut oil

1 tablespoon chia seeds

3 tablespoons raw cacao powder

1 tablespoon lucuma powder

Pinch of sea salt

1 tablespoon vanilla extract

2 tablespoons coconut syrup or
    maple syrup

Method

1 Place the nuts in a food processor and process until very fine. Add the remaining ingredients and process to combine them into a dough. If the mixture is too dry add a splash of water.

2 Take walnut-size pieces of the dough and press into cookie shapes. These can be refrigerated and eaten soft or you can dehydrate the cookies in a dehydrator for 6 hours. Flip the cookies over and dehydrate for another 6 hours until crisp.

RICH IN ANTIOXIDANTS	
Calories (per serving)	172
Protein	4.6 g
Total fat	11.5 g
of which saturated fat	2.6 g
Carbohydrates	12.5 g
of which sugars	8.1 g
Vitamins/minerals E, B, copper, manganese	

Herb and Tomato Flaxseed Crackers

HIGH FIBER

These low-calorie crackers are perfect to eat as a snack or with dips for lunch. Vary the flavors according to taste. For sweet crackers, blend mixed berries and dried dates with the flaxseeds.

Prep: 20 mins/Dry: 12 hrs

Ingredients
(makes around 20 crackers)

Generous 1 cup (200 g) whole flaxseed

¾ cup (100 g) sunflower seeds

3 tomatoes, chopped

2 sundried tomatoes, chopped

3 tablespoons lemon juice

1 teaspoon dried mixed herbs

½ teaspoon garlic powder

½ teaspoon sea salt or garlic salt

⅔ cup (150 ml) water

Method

1 Grind the flaxseed and sunflower seeds in a food processor until fine. Add the remaining ingredients and blend to form a stiff paste, adding enough water to create a thick spreadable batter.

2 Spread the batter, about ¼ in (½ cm) thick onto nonstick dehydrator sheets or on nonstick baking sheets. Shape the batter into a large square and score lines into the batter to make individual crackers.

3 Dehydrate at 115°F (46°C) for 5 to 6 hours then flip over and dry for another 6 hours until dry and crispy. Break into individual crackers along the score lines. These can be stored in an airtight container for up to a week.

GREAT FOR DIGESTION AND BONES	
Calories (per serving)	87
Protein	2.9 g
Total fat	6.9 g
of which saturated fat	0.8 g
Carbohydrates	4.2 g
of which sugars	0.7 g
Vitamins/minerals	B, iron, calcium

Fermented Foods

Fermented foods have been around for thousands of years. They are not only an effective way to preserve foods but they also provide beneficial bacteria for our guts, which is important for overall health.

Fermented foods are naturally rich in a wide range of live beneficial or "friendly" bacteria and yeasts called probiotics. Consuming them daily is an excellent way to ensure a healthy gut as they help to restore the natural balance of intestinal flora, especially when it has been disrupted after taking antibiotics. Many fermented foods are drinks, such as Kombucha (see page 158), Water Kefir (see page 197), and milk kefir. Others are used as condiments, like sauerkraut, miso soup, and kimchi, or used in sweet and savory dishes, such as yogurt. For those avoiding dairy foods kefir and yogurt can be made using nut milks (see page 154) and coconut milk instead of dairy products.

Probiotics are known to have many benefits including improving digestion, supporting the immune system, lowering inflammation, and protecting against microbial infections.

Health Benefits of Fermented Foods

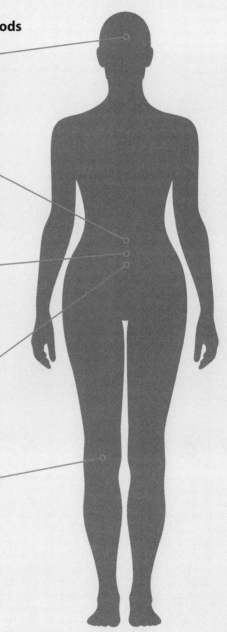

 Brain health: A healthy gut flora has been shown to be important for brain function and influencing mood. Probiotics affect the central nervous system (CNS) and the balance of neurotransmitters such as gamma-aminobutyric acid (GABA), which creates a sense of calm, so reducing anxiety.

 Immune system: It is estimated that around 70–80 percent of the body's immune system is contained within the gut. By nourishing it with beneficial bacteria you can keep the immune system healthy and lower inflammation.

 Digestive health: Beneficial bacteria play a vital role in the production and absorption of key nutrients such as B vitamins. They help ease and improve digestion and protect the body from harmful pathogens.

Healthy weight: Your gut flora also plays a large role in your metabolism. A healthy gut flora has been shown to help maintain a healthy weight. Many fermented foods, such as sauerkraut, are also low in calories and high in fiber helping to keep you feeling fuller for much longer.

 Bone health: One of the benefits of probiotic bacteria is their ability to produce vitamin K_2, which plays a vital role in maintaining healthy bones. Milk kefir and yogurt also provide calcium that is important for bones.

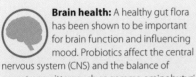

Fermented Foods

There are a number of fermented foods that can be made at home or purchased at the grocery or health food store. It is always important to choose raw fermented foods and drinks as processing and heating will destroy the beneficial bacteria. Pickled foods are not the same as fermented foods, unless it is stated on the label.

Nutrition: Fermented foods are full of enzymes, vitamins, minerals, and beneficial probiotics.

Benefits: Introduce healthy and good bacteria to the digestive system, helping you to absorb nutrients better.

Foods that you ferment yourself can last for many months and also provide an ideal way to preserve vegetables. For the best health benefits, always select good-quality organic produce to ferment.

If you have never eaten fermented foods before, start with just a spoonful at a time to enable your intestinal flora to adjust to the new bacteria, then gradually increase the amount—it is recommended to eat ¼ to ½ cup daily for optimal health.

Sauerkraut

Traditionally, sauerkraut is made from fermented cabbage, although other vegetables can also be added.

- High in fiber and low in calories, sauerkraut is ideal for weight loss.
- Sauerkraut is rich in vitamins C, A, K, various B vitamins, and iron to provide quick energy, help prevent anemia, and also boost circulation.

Kimchi

A spicy Korean condiment made from fermented cabbage, radish, and flavored with a mixture of garlic, salt, vinegar, chili, and other spices.

- Kimchi is beneficial for promoting digestion when served with meals.
- An excellent source of vitamins A and C, as well as healthy bacteria to support the immune system.

Nut Yogurt

If you are avoiding dairy products you can purchase or make yogurt made from nuts. You can use any nut milk as a base for making your own yogurt (see page 154).

- Almond yogurt is rich in vitamin E to keep the skin healthy.
- Nut yogurts provide a good source of protein, heart-healthy fats, fiber, and lots of antioxidants.

Coconut Yogurt

A popular dairy-free yogurt, coconut yogurt is available from grocery and health food stores or is also easy to make yourself.

- Rich in lauric acid, coconut yogurt helps to support the immune system.
- Coconut yogurt contains medium chain triglycerides (MCT), which can be preferentially burned as a fuel, making it useful for boosting energy levels.

Homemade Almond Yogurt

PROBIOTIC

Making your own rich and creamy nut yogurt is healthy and cheaper than buying ready-made varieties. Any nuts can be used but almonds are particularly good. To reduce enzyme inhibitors, soak the nuts for at least 12 hours. You can use a yogurt starter kit or probiotic powder to inoculate the yogurt with beneficial bacteria.

Prep: 30 mins/Soak: 12 hrs/
Ferment: 9 to 12 hrs

Ingredients (serves 4)

Generous ¾ cup (125 g) raw almonds,
  soaked in filtered water for 12 hours
2 cups (500 ml) coconut water
1 tablespoon coconut sugar
½ teaspoon probiotic powder

Method

1 Preheat the oven to 275°F (140°C, gas mark 1). Sterilize a glass jar by washing in hot soapy water, rinsing, and placing in the oven to dry completely.

2 Place all the ingredients in a blender and process until smooth and creamy. Pour into the sterilized glass jar and leave in a warm room for 9 to 12 hours to ferment. After this time it should taste slightly sour.

3 Serve immediately, or cover the yogurt with a sterilized lid and store in the refrigerator for up to a week.

GREAT FOR THE IMMUNE SYSTEM	
Calories (per serving)	229
Protein	7.5 g
Total fat	17.7 g
of which saturated fat	1.4 g
Carbohydrates	10.4 g
of which sugars	4.1 g
Vitamins/minerals	E, B, iron, calcium

Water Kefir

Kefir is an ancient cultured food that is hydrating and refreshing. Water kefir is made using water kefir grains (sugar and live cultures) fermented in a sugared water or coconut water (see page 197).

- Rich in enzymes and several strains of friendly bacteria and yeasts, which can dramatically improve digestion and keep the immune system healthy.

Milk and Coconut Kefir

This delicious probiotic drink is energizing and a good source of protein and healthy fats. It can be made from coconut milk.

- Kefir contains minerals, such as calcium (milk kefir), magnesium, and B vitamins, to build bone density.
- Kefir helps to restore a healthy digestive system and alleviates bloating, constipation, and diarrhea.

Kombucha

Known as the "immortal health elixir" by the ancient Chinese, kombucha has been consumed for more than 2,000 years. It is made from sweetened tea that's been fermented by a symbiotic colony of bacteria and yeast (known as SCOBY).

- Rich in many of the enzymes the body produces for digestion, kombucha aids cleansing and supports liver health.

Why Eat Pickles?

Homemade pickled vegetables are a wonderful way to preserve ripe produce and if left to ferment also provide plenty of beneficial bacteria. Store-bought pickled vegetables are typically not fermented and do not provide probiotic bacteria.

Homemade pickled vegetables are low in calories and high in fiber making them ideal for healthy weight management, lowering cholesterol, and supporting blood sugar balance. All the vitamins, minerals, and fiber of the vegetable are retained during the pickling process.

Many store-bought pickles use vinegar rather than traditionally salting. Without natural fermentation the live bacteria cultures that turn pickles into a healthy probiotic food are absent. Most vegetables can be pickled and for additional benefits and flavor, spices such as turmeric and garlic or herbs can be added.

To make your own pickle, dissolve sea salt in water, wash your organic vegetables, and chop into pieces. Tightly pack the vegetables, herbs, and spices into a sterilized jar (see page 154) and pour over the salt water solution (brine). The liquid should cover the vegetables. Set the lid loosely on top of the jar, don't seal it, and let the jar sit undisturbed at room temperature. You'll know fermentation has begun when you see bubbles rising to the top of the jar and the water becomes cloudy. It generally takes between three to ten days before the pickle is done. Taste the pickle during this time to see if it is ready. It should have a tangy but not sour flavor. Once fermented store in the refrigerator for up to a week. Eat in moderation as the pickle is relatively high in salt.

Kombucha

LOW CALORIE

A delicious refreshing drink. You can use any tea for the base of your kombucha although green tea works particularly well. You can vary the flavorings—for example by adding lemon or lime to the brew. Do not use metal equipment or utensils when making kefir or kombucha as it reacts with the metal—use wooden or plastic spoons and bowls. The starter SCOBY can be purchased online. The level of sugar and calories will vary depending on the length of fermentation.

Prep: 10 mins/Cool: 1 hr/
Ferment: 3 to 14 days

Ingredients

4 to 6 green tea tea bags or 1½ tablespoons loose-leaf tea
Scant 1 cup (170 g) superfine or granulated sugar or coconut sugar
1 package of kombucha starter culture (SCOBY)
Orange or lemon slices, optional

AIDS DIGESTION AND DETOXIFICATION	
Calories (per 100 g)	13
Protein	0 g
Total fat	0 g
of which saturated fat	0 g
Carbohydrates	3.0 g
of which sugars	1.0 g
Vitamins/minerals	beneficial bacteria

Method

1 Put the tea bags into a large sterilized glass container (see page 154) and add the sugar. Pour over 3 cups (750 ml) boiling water, stir well, and let cool for 1 hour, or until it reaches room temperature.

2 Add the SCOBY, cover the container with a cloth or cheesecloth, and leave in a warm place for three to 14 days—this will depend on the temperature of the room. The liquid will become cloudy when ready. After three days, taste the brew. If it tastes fruity and not tealike, it is ready, if not, leave it another day and try again.

3 Strain, but leave a little of the tea in the container with the SCOBY while you make another batch to repeat the process. Keep the ready-made brew in the refrigerator for three to four days.

Healthy Fats and Oils

Raw plant fats such as avocados, olives, coconuts, nuts, and seeds are an essential part of a healthy raw food diet.

Healthy plant fats contain lots of antioxidants which help to protect the oils from being oxidized, otherwise they will go rancid quickly. A variety of these fats should be included in your daily diet to provide enough calories, fat soluble vitamins, and essential fats to support cell health, keep the brain functioning, moisturize the skin and hair, and help support the immune system.

Always choose natural unrefined olive, vegetable, nut, and seed oils that have been cold pressed at low temperatures to prevent oxidation when exposed to the air and free radical damage. Many oils react to light so, once opened, they should be stored in the refrigerator and used within two months. Flaxseed oil, once opened, should be kept in the refrigerator and used within six weeks, and cold-pressed olive oil should be stored in a cool dark place for up to six to eight weeks before the phytonutrient and antioxidant content of the oil becomes depleted.

Health Benefits of Fats and Oils

Brain health: Certain fats such as flaxseed and hemp oil provide omega-3 fatty acids to support brain function and boost mood. Coconut oil, rich in medium chain triglycerides (MCT), has been shown to help boost cognitive function and may reduce the risk of dementia.

Dental health: Coconut oil and sesame oil are traditionally used in oil pulling. Oil pulling is an Ayurvedic Indian tradition that has been around for thousands of years and involves swishing a tablespoon of oil around in the mouth for 20 minutes then spitting it out. Oil pulling has been shown to reduce plaque, cavity-causing bacteria, and bad breath while improving gum health.

Heart health: Fats such as avocado oil and flaxseed oil contain healthy monounsaturated fats and omega-3 fatty acids that help lower inflammation and keep the heart healthy. These fats also help to lower LDL cholesterol and triglycerides.

Immune system: Certain oils such as coconut oil are known to support the immune system and are rich in antiviral and antimicrobial properties. Omega-3 fatty acids, such as flaxseed and chia oil, help lower inflammation and keep the immune system healthy.

Skin health: Including enough monounsaturated and omega-3 fatty acids in the diet can keep the skin healthy. Adding fat to plant foods also supports the absorption of fat soluble vitamins A, D, E, and K along with antioxidants like carotenoids. Carotenoids help to protect the skin from UV damage.

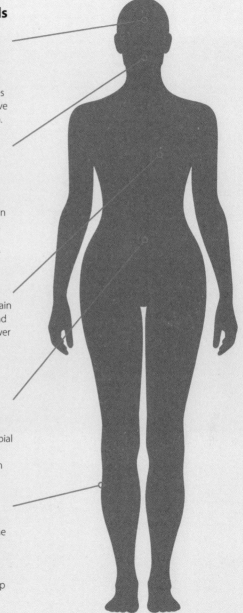

Pumpkin Seed Oil

This oil is made by pressing raw pumpkin seeds. It has a rich nutty flavor and is a great addition to salads or raw soups.

- Pumpkin seed oil has traditionally been used to treat intestinal parasites.
- This oil has a very high fatty acid content and is good for reducing inflammation for irritable bowel (IBS) sufferers.
- Pumpkin seed oil lubricates joints.

Avocado Oil

Avocado oil is pressed from the fruit of the avocado. It can be used topically on the skin as well as internally.

- Rich in antioxidant vitamin E, avocado oil has protective properties for the skin and heart and is useful for supporting the immune system.
- Avocado oil contains fatty acids to help maintain healthy cholesterol levels.

Olive Oil

The quality of olive oil influences its health benefits. Extra virgin olive oil is particularly rich in antioxidants and effective at lowering inflammation.

- Olive oil is beneficial for keeping the heart healthy and supporting blood vessels due to the presence of antioxidants like vitamin E.
- Olive oil may have anticancer benefits.

Flaxseed Oil

Flaxseed oil is made from crushed flaxseeds and is available as both liquid and soft gel capsules.

- Flaxseed oil appears to reduce the risk of certain cancers including prostate cancer.
- Rich in omega-3 fatty acids, flaxseed oil helps to lower blood pressure and can also boost mood.

Hemp Seed Oil

Hemp seed oil has a pleasant nutty flavor, so is ideal in dressings and dips.

- Hemp seed oil contains a good balance of omega-3 and -6 fatty acids and is easily digestible making it very good for skin conditions.
- The oleic acid (omega-9) and omega-3 fatty acids in the oil lower inflammation and keep the heart healthy.

Sesame Oil

Sesame seed oil contains vitamin K and traces of magnesium, which are important to boost bone density.

- High in monounsaturated fats, sesame oil can be beneficial for heart health.
- Sesame oil contains vitamin E to help the immune system to function well.
- This oil may prevent tooth decay as it contains antibacterial properties.

Macadamia Nut Oil

With a rich buttery flavor, this oil is delicious in salad dressings.

- Macadamia nut oil is high in monounsaturated fats and contains omega-3 fatty acids while being low in omega-6, which makes it particularly useful for lowering inflammation, reducing cholesterol levels, and helping to clean the arteries.

Chia Seed Oil

An excellent source of omega-3 fatty acids, chia seed oil is valuable topically as a skin moisturizer to keep the skin hydrated, and internally to support cell health and keep the brain functioning well.

- Chia seed oil is beneficial for inflammatory conditions.
- This oil can improve absorption of fat-soluble vitamins when added to dishes.

Walnut Oil

A good source of anti-inflammatory omega-3 fatty acids, which are excellent for keeping the brain healthy, walnut oil is also rich in manganese and copper to keep bones strong.

- Walnut oil offers an extremely good source of antioxidants, specifically ellagic acid, which is known for its anticancer properties.

Red Pepper and Walnut Dip

HEALTHY SKIN

This easy pantry dip or spread takes just minutes to make. Rich in antioxidants and essential fats, the addition of walnut oil gives it a wonderful fruity flavor. Serve the dip with vegetable sticks or raw seed crackers (see page 148).

Prep: 8 mins

Ingredients (serves 6)

Pinch of paprika

1 garlic clove, crushed

1 cup (100 g) walnuts, chopped

1 red bell pepper

4 sundried tomatoes

3 tablespoons walnut oil

1 tablespoon balsamic vinegar

2 teaspoons coconut syrup or yacon syrup

Salt and freshly ground black pepper

Method

1 Place all the ingredients in a blender or food processor and blend until smooth. Season to taste. This dip will keep in the refrigerator for up to three to four days.

BURSTING WITH ANTIOXIDANTS	
Calories (per serving)	212
Protein	2.8 g
Total fat	20.7 g
of which saturated fat	2.2 g
Carbohydrates	3.5 g
of which sugars	3.0 g
Vitamins/minerals	B, A, C, copper

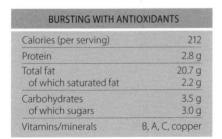

Asian Dressing

LOW CARB

This is a delicious dressing for raw salads particularly if poured over dark leafy greens. You can also use this as a dipping sauce for raw sushi rolls (see page 78) and as a marinade for vegetables, which can then be dehydrated.

Prep: 5 mins

Ingredients

2 tablespoons minced shallot

3 tablespoons tamari soy sauce

2 tablespoons rice vinegar

1 teaspoon coconut syrup or sugar

1 teaspoon grated fresh ginger root

1 tablespoon sesame oil

1 tablespoon flaxseed oil

1 teaspoon sesame seeds

Salt and freshly ground black pepper

Method

1 Place all the ingredients in a large salad bowl and mix together thoroughly.

2 Serve the dressing alongside mixed salads or use as a dipping sauce for raw nori rolls. This dressing will keep in the refrigerator for three to four days.

GOOD SOURCE OF OMEGA-3 FATTY ACIDS	
Calories (per tablespoon)	40
Protein	0.3 g
Total fat	3.6 g
of which saturated fat	0.4 g
Carbohydrates	1.2 g
of which sugars	0.9 g
Vitamins/minerals	E, K

Why Eat Coconut?

Coconuts are one of the most nutritious and incredibly versatile fruits. Fresh coconuts can be consumed young or mature. Young coconuts have either a green shell or a white "husk" if the outer shell has been removed, while mature coconuts are brown. The nutritional content changes as a coconut matures: young coconuts have more "water" and a soft, gel-like flesh, while mature coconuts have firm meat and less liquid.

Coconut Oil

Coconut oil is the fatty oil that comes from the coconut meat. The quality of oil varies, but choose organic virgin coconut oil to obtain the most health benefits. It is rich in lauric acid, which is known for being antiviral, antibacterial, and antifungal. It is also rich in medium chain triglycerides (MCT), which are easily digested by the body for boosting energy and brain function.

Coconut Meat

Fresh coconut meat is low in carbohydrate and a good source of fiber. High in fats, it is very sustaining and helpful for balancing blood sugar levels. Coconut meat is available shredded, which is mostly dry and comes in thin strips, flaked (wider, flatter strips), and dry unsweetened. Choose unsweetened products to avoid additional sugars.

Coconut Aminos

Coconut aminos is a soy-free seasoning sauce made from the coconut tree sap. This sap has a very low glycemic index (GI) and is an abundant source of amino acids, minerals, vitamin C, and B vitamins. It can be used to replace soy sauce in dishes, dressings, and dips.

Coconut Milk

Made from the expressed juice of grated coconut meat and water, the fat content of coconut milk varies— both whole and light versions are available. It is a useful source of fiber to balance blood sugar levels, while the fat content helps to keep you feeling full. It also contains bone supporting minerals, such as magnesium, phosphorus, and manganese.

Coconut Cream

This is made from pressing the coconut meat. Choose unsweetened brands. A high fat food, it adds flavor and a creamy texture to Asian dishes.

Coconut Berry Chia Pudding

HIGH ENERGY

This is a delicious dessert or breakfast option. Using coconut milk creates a wonderful creamy, satisfying dish to help energize the body. Frozen mixed berries or cherries make a delicious topping for the chia pudding.

Prep: 10 mins/Chill: 4 to 6 hrs

Ingredients (serves 2)

1¼ cups (300 ml) whole coconut milk
2 teaspoons vanilla extract
5 tablespoons chia seeds
7 oz (200 g) frozen mixed berries, thawed
1 tablespoon maple syrup

Method

1 Combine the coconut milk, vanilla, and chia seeds in a bowl. Stir well then refrigerate for 4 to 6 hours or overnight until the mixture is thick.

2 Place the berries and maple syrup in a food processor and pulse a couple of times to form a compote.

3 Divide the chia pudding between two glasses and top with the fruit compote to serve.

GOOD FOR BALANCING BLOOD SUGAR	
Calories (per serving)	261
Protein	7.8 g
Total fat	12.4 g
of which saturated fat	1.5 g
Carbohydrates	32.3 g
of which sugars	15.7 g
Vitamins/minerals	C, K, zinc, calcium

Raw Pantry

If you're looking to follow the raw food diet and adopt the raw food lifestyle, then it is worth spending some time clearing out your pantry and stocking it with some healthy raw food staples.

There are a range of nutritious pantry ingredients that can help to transform raw dishes instantly adding flavor, texture, and additional nutrients. While not all of these products are strictly raw they are all valuable additions in a raw food kitchen.

Key products include nuts and seeds, grains, seasonings and condiments (vinegars, cold-pressed oils, nutritional yeast), flavorings (tahini, tamari, cinnamon), sweeteners (date, yacon syrup), superfoods (cacao, goji berries, maca), drinks (coconut water and herbal teas), and dried goods (fruit, sea vegetables, dried mushrooms). Keeping your pantry well stocked means that you can create delicious raw dishes at a moment's notice, but you don't need to go out and buy everything all at once. Just start with the basics and then build the rest up gradually. When choosing pantry products select those that have been minimally processed and/or are organic.

Health Benefits of Pantry Foods

 Anti-inflammatory: Many spices, such as turmeric, garlic, and cayenne, are known for their powerful anti-inflammatory properties, making them ideal for relieving inflammatory conditions like arthritis and asthma.

 Heart health: Certain pantry ingredients like nutritional yeast flakes and royal jelly contain a range of nutrients, including B vitamins, that are good for keeping the heart and cardiovascular system healthy.

 Blood sugar: Condiments such as vinegar can lower the blood sugar response after eating, improving insulin function, and even your feeling of fullness when taken before or during a meal. Ground cinnamon and vanilla extract are also beneficial spices for keeping blood sugar levels under control.

 Digestive health: Some pantry ingredients like miso paste and yacon syrup are rich in digestible fibers that encourage bowel regularity and provide prebiotic fibers to boost levels of beneficial bacteria in our gut.

 Joint health: Vinegars such as apple cider vinegar and balsamic vinegar contain calcium, magnesium, potassium, and phosphorus, which are all essential minerals for relieving joint pain in inflammatory conditions like arthritis, as well as helping to keep bones healthy.

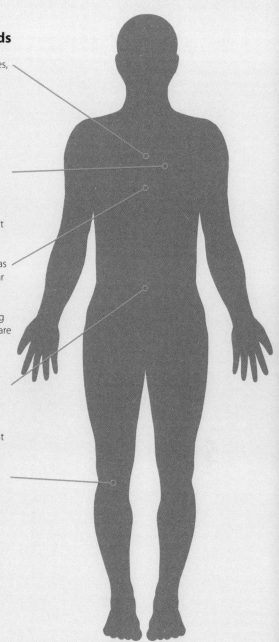

Seasonings and Condiments

A variety of seasonings and condiments will enhance the flavor of raw food dishes and also add some useful health benefits. Vinegar is great added to salad dressings, and spices (such as vanilla and cinnamon) give a tasty lift to breakfasts and desserts. Nutritional yeast flakes create a rich flavor base when added to many raw dishes.

Nutrition: A variety of seasonings and condiments add flavor and extra health benefits to raw food dishes.
Benefits: Lower blood pressure, keep the nervous system functioning, and promote healthy skin and bones.

Apple Cider Vinegar

Organic, unfiltered apple cider vinegar contains "mother" strands of proteins, enzymes, and friendly bacteria that give the vinegar a cloudy appearance.

- Apple cider vinegar has been shown to improve insulin sensitivity and lower blood sugar responses after meals.
- This vinegar can promote digestion before a meal.

Balsamic Vinegar

Balsamic vinegar is an aromatic vinegar prepared from pressed grape juice.

- Balsamic vinegar is a source of polyphenol antioxidants, to protect the body from the harmful effects of free radicals.
- The acetic acid in balsamic vinegar helps to improve the absorption of calcium to strengthen bones and teeth.

Nama Shoyu

Nama shoyu is a raw soy sauce. Made from fermented soybeans, its rich flavor comes from an abundance of amino acids derived from soy protein.

- Naturally gluten free, Nama shoyu adds a salty taste to dishes.
- Nama shoyu is a good source of vitamin B_3, protein, manganese, and tryptophan, an amino acid that can boost mood.

Miso

Miso is a fermented soybean paste and is a good source of manganese, copper, zinc, and phosphorus.

- Rich in a range of phytonutrients known for their antioxidant and anti-inflammatory properties.
- Miso contains microorganisms such as *Aspergillus oryzae*, which help digestion and the absorption of nutrients.

Nutritional Yeast Flakes

Nutritional yeast is deactivated yeast and is a great source of nutrition. It is generally used as a condiment to add a cheeselike flavor to dishes.

- Nutritional yeast is a complete protein and is particularly rich in the B vitamins. Some brands are fortified with B_{12}, making it beneficial on a raw food diet.
- This is also a great source of folic acid.

Celtic/Himalayan Sea Salt

Celtic sea salt is similar to Himalayan crystal salt in its composition and health benefits. It is naturally harvested in Brittany, France, near the Celtic Sea. Himalayan salt is unrefined, unprocessed raw salt mined from salt caves.

- Rich in numerous trace minerals to support a healthy electrolyte balance, helping to prevent muscle cramps.

Tahini

Tahini is a paste made from ground sesame seeds. It is extremely versatile and can be used in both sweet and savory dishes.

- Packed with the minerals phosphorus, calcium, lecithin, and magnesium, tahini is ideal for keeping bones strong.
- Tahini is a good source of protein and vitamin E to prevent heart disease.

Vanilla

Vanilla has a long history of use as an antioxidant and cognitive enhancing spice. Choose fresh beans or pure extract as vanilla flavor can be artificially made and the quality is not as high as pure extract.

- Vanilla is rich in chemicals called vanilloids that help reduce inflammation and improve mental performance.
- Vanilla can calm stomach pains.

Why Eat Cinnamon?

Cinnamon is a very popular culinary and medicinal spice used for adding aromatic flavor to a wide range of dishes. It contains a substance called cinnamaldehyde, which is responsible for most of its health benefits.

- Rich in antioxidants that have anti-inflammatory effects, cinnamon has been shown to increase sensitivity and improve blood sugar balance. It can also help in the fight against fungal and bacterial infections.
- Cinnamon may have beneficial effects on neurodegenerative conditions such as Alzheimer's.
- Cinnamon is an excellent source of calcium, manganese, and fiber. The combination of calcium and fiber helps to bind bile acids and eliminate them from the body, which in turn helps to lower cholesterol levels. The fiber also helps to relieve constipation and diarrhea, so is helpful for IBS sufferers.

Sweeteners

Refined sugar is associated with numerous chronic diseases—like diabetes—and so should be avoided in a raw food diet. However, there are options for adding sweetness to dishes other than using fresh or dried fruit. If you wish to add sweetness to your diet, here are some healthier choices to use instead of refined sugar.

Nutrition: Most natural sweeteners are low in calories, low in fructose, and also taste sweet.

Benefits: May lower blood pressure, improve bone density, and help to prevent tooth decay.

Xylitol

Xylitol is a sugar alcohol typically derived from birch trees. It is often added to products such as toothpaste and chewing gum as it can reduce dental decay.

- With 40 percent less calories than table sugar it has a low glycemic index (GI) so does not upset blood sugar levels.
- Excess xylitol can cause abdominal gas and diarrhea so use in small amounts.

Erythritol

Erythritol is another sugar alcohol but contains virtually no calories, has a low glycemic index (GI), a low laxative effect, and is very sweet. It is available in granulated form and can be used in recipes to replace ordinary table sugar.

- Erythritol does not affect glucose and insulin levels, making it useful for people suffering from diabetes.

Stevia

Stevia is a sweet herb from the leaf of the South American stevia plant. It is intensely sweet so use in very small amounts to sweeten dishes and drinks. It is available as a powder, tablet, and liquid.

- Stevia has no calories so, depending on how it is used, it can help with weight management. It contains vitamins A, C, and B, and also iron, zinc, and calcium.

Lo Han Guo

Lo han guo is another natural sweetener similar to stevia. In China, the lo han guo fruit has been used to add sweetness to foods for centuries. It's about 200 times sweeter than sugar, so only use in minute amounts, but has zero calories. Available as a powder.

- Lo han guo is good for weight loss.
- It does not contribute to tooth decay.

Coconut Sugar

This sugar is made from the sap, (the sugary fluid), of the coconut plant. It is also referred to as coconut palm sugar and is similar to table sugar so is not a low-calorie alternative.

- Coconut sugar has a relatively low GI.
- This sugar contains traces of certain nutrients including iron, zinc, calcium, and potassium.

Yacon Syrup

Yacon syrup comes from the yacon tuber, an Andean crop that's commonly eaten like potatoes in South America. It is a sweet syrup that tastes a bit like molasses and has a low glycemic index (GI).

- Yacon syrup is rich in inulin that acts as a prebiotic fiber, making it helpful for digestion. Its slight laxative effect reduces constipation.

Palmyra Jaggery

Palmyra jaggery is the unrefined sugar made from the sap tapped from palmyra trees. Palmyra jaggery is thought to be the most nutritious sweetener, it has a sweet caramel flavor, and a relatively low GI score of around 40.

- Palmyra jaggery contains numerous vitamins and minerals including iron, B_6, calcium, potassium, and B_{12}.

Maple Syrup

Maple syrup is the boiled and refined sap of maple trees and has a GI of 54. It has been studied for its antioxidant properties but as yet there is little research to show its clinical significance for human health.

- Maple syrup contains some manganese, iron, and calcium but in terms of nutrition it is not significantly different from white sugar.

Why Eat Bee Products?

While bee products are not consumed on a vegan diet, some people following a raw food diet do include them to add flavor and extra nutrients to many dishes. Bee products have been very popular for thousands of years and are renowned for their energizing and healing properties.

Bee Pollen

Bee pollen is made from millions of microscopic pollen grains that are collected by bees and bound together with nectar. Rich in amino acids, energizing B vitamins, antioxidants, and vitamins C and A, it also contains a wealth of essential minerals. Available as granules in health food stores.

Honey

A natural sweetener, raw unprocessed honey and Manuka honey contain a wealth of enzymes that can aid digestion. Honey is known for its antimicrobial properties and is rich in antioxidants. Use in small amounts to avoid upsetting blood sugar balance.

Propolis

Propolis is a substance collected by honey bees from trees and buds and used as a sealant in their hive. Known to support the immune system, it is rich in antimicrobial compounds making it useful for fighting infections. Available as capsules and tinctures from health food stores.

Royal Jelly

Royal jelly is secreted by the nurse bee's hypopharyngeal glands and is fed to selected larvae for the first four days of their growth cycle. It contains lots of B vitamins and is traditionally considered to be a brain food and energy tonic. It also helps to keep the adrenals healthy and to relieve stress. Available as a powder or capsules from health food stores.

Honey Pistachio Halva

HIGH ENERGY

A rich indulgent dessert packed with protein and healthy fats from the tahini. You can vary the nuts according to taste and also add a spoonful of superberry powder if you want to give it an additional antioxidant boost.

Prep: 15 mins/Freeze: 1 to 2 hrs

Ingredients (makes 10 slices)
½ cup (120 g) tahini
4 tablespoons coconut sugar, ground up
 very fine
2 tablespoons raw honey or maple syrup
1 teaspoon vanilla extract
1 teaspoon lucuma powder
3 tablespoons pistachios, coarsely
 chopped
3 tablespoons dry unsweetened coconut

Method

1 Place the tahini, coconut sugar, honey, and vanilla in a bowl and beat the mixture well.

2 Add the lucuma, nuts, and coconut to the mixture and beat them until they are fully combined.

3 Line a small loaf pan with plastic wrap and press the mixture into the pan.

4 Freeze for 1 to 2 hours until the halva is firm, then cut it into slices to serve.

EXCELLENT FOR BONES	
Calories (per serving)	165
Protein	3.3 g
Total fat	12.4 g
of which saturated fat	3.7 g
Carbohydrates	10.6 g
of which sugars	8.6 g
Vitamins/minerals	B, calcium, iron, zinc

Vegan Tart with Creamy Cheese Filling

HIGH PROTEIN

These delicious tartlets are rich and creamy, and make a tasty dinner when served with salad. The filling includes sundried tomatoes and onion but you could also blend in herbs or olives for additional flavor.

Prep: 30 mins/Soak: 2 hrs/ Dry: 4 hrs

Ingredients (makes 4 tarts)

¾ cup (115 g) whole flaxseeds
Generous ¾ cup (125 g) cashews, ideally soaked for 2 hours then drained
1 small zucchini, chopped
½ teaspoon sea salt
2 tablespoons nutritional yeast flakes
4 tablespoons coconut oil, melted

Filling

Scant ½ cup (60 g) macadamias
Scant ½ cup (60 g) cashews
2 tablespoons nutritional yeast flakes
1 tablespoon tamari or Nama shoyu
2 teaspoons lemon juice
3 or 4 tablespoons water
1 shallot, diced
4 sundried tomatoes, finely chopped
Slices of cherry tomatoes, diced onion, and chopped parsley, to garnish

Method

1 Grind the flaxseeds and cashews in a blender or food processor until fine.

2 Place the zucchini, sea salt, yeast flakes, and oil in a blender and process until smooth. Add to the ground nuts and mix to form a dough, adding a little water if needed to bind it together. Line 4 mini tartlet pans with plastic wrap and press the mixture into the pans.

3 Place the tartlet shells in a dehydrator or warm oven at 113°F (45°C) and dry for 4 hours or until dry at the edges.

BALANCES BLOOD SUGAR LEVELS	
Calories (per tart)	675
Protein	19.4 g
Total fat	58.0 g
of which saturated fat	15.4 g
Carbohydrates	20.9 g
of which sugars	4.4 g
Vitamins/minerals	B, C, zinc, copper

4 To make the filling, place the nuts, yeast flakes, tamari, lemon juice, and water in a blender and process to form a thick paste, adding a little more water if needed. Stir in the shallot and tomatoes.

5 Spoon the filling into the shells and top with slices of tomato, diced onion, and chopped parsley to serve.

Beverages

One of the benefits of a raw food diet is that it is naturally hydrating. Fruits and vegetables, for example, contain plenty of water and electrolytes to replenish lost fluids and essential minerals.

Drinking enough water is still important to cleanse and hydrate the body and help in the absorption of nutrients. Filtered water is best as the contaminants that may be present in ordinary drinking water have been removed. Use filtered water when making nut milks, juices, and smoothies.

Including antioxidant-rich herbal teas, green juices, and smoothies or nut and seed milks is another easy way to cram additional nutrients such as fiber, protein, vitamins, and minerals into your diet. Fermented drinks like kombucha, water kefir, and coconut kefir are also recommended to provide the body with plenty of friendly bacteria, essential for a healthy immune system and to support overall digestive health.

Other drinks, such as green tea and chaga tea, are known for their energizing and cancer-protective properties due to the powerful antioxidants they contain. Green tea in particular may also help in weight loss and boost concentration.

Health Benefits of Beverages

 **Brain health:** Keeping the body hydrated is essential for cognitive function and mood. Certain drinks such as herbal teas and green teas can also improve focus and concentration.

Detoxification: Many drinks included on a raw food diet, such as green juices and smoothies, help with detoxification by removing impurities from the body and improving liver function. Smoothies provide plenty of fiber too, which is important for a healthy digestive system and cleansing.

Anticancer: Freshly pressed juices and smoothies are packed with antioxidants known to help protect the body from carcinogens. Other drinks such as green tea are known for their anticancer properties.

 Healthy weight: By kick-starting the day with a green smoothie or nut milk shake you can keep the body feeling satisfied for longer due to their fiber and protein content. This can help balance blood sugars, reduce cravings, and help you maintain a healthy weight.

 Energy levels: Keeping the body hydrated is essential for energy levels. Green juices and smoothies provide plenty of key vitamins and minerals to support energy production. Other drinks, such as coconut water, provide essential electrolytes, which are often lost via sweat during exercise.

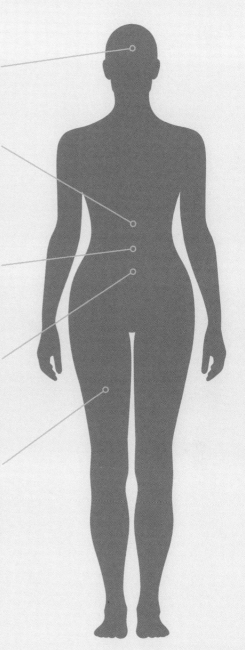

Water

Water is the primary drink of choice as it reduces your appetite, making it great for weight loss. It also flushes toxins out of the body so it helps to keep the skin clear and prevent urinary infections and kidney stones. If you find regular water boring then try sparkling water or add a squeeze of lime or lemon juice for additional flavor.

Nutrition: Water contains zero calories, is low in sodium, and may contain traces of calcium and fluoride. **Benefits:** Maintains the body's fluid balance and helps with concentration and clear thinking.

Coconut Water

Coconut water is the water from young, immature coconuts.

- Coconut water is a powerhouse of electrolytes, vitamins, minerals, and phytonutrients, and is low in sugar, so may prevent urinary tract infections.
- As a natural isotonic drink, coconut water is great for postexercise rehydration.
- Coconut water is useful for digestion.

Maple Water

Maple water is the extracted sap from maple trees and is naturally low in calories.

- Maple water is a sweet, naturally filtered water, containing a number of minerals, such as calcium, potassium, magnesium, and manganese, which are good for the heart and kidneys.
- Maple water is quite low in sugar so can be a hydrating drink.

Teas

You can drink normal black tea on a raw food diet. Black tea can also be used to make iced drinks and smoothies blended with nut milks. Tea not only rehydrates, but can also protect against heart disease and some cancers. Green tea, however, is much richer in antioxidants than black tea because it is not as processed.

Nutrition: Tea contains antioxidant flavonoids and polyphenols, as well as other beneficial phytochemicals. **Benefits:** Can help with weight loss, cardiovascular health, and improves bone strength.

Black Tea

Black tea has less caffeine than coffee and provides a variety of health benefits including antioxidant, anticarcinogenic, and anti-inflammatory properties.

- The polyphenols in black tea can help oral health by restricting the bacteria that causes tooth decay.
- Black tea contains the amino acid L-theanine, which has a calming effect.

Herbal Teas

Herbal teas are delicious either hot or cold. Made from herbs or fruit extracts, some have specific health benefits.

- Certain calming herbs to use include valerian, camomile, or lemon balm.
- Adaptogenic herbs are also popular, including tulsi, licorice, and ginseng.
- Peppermint, marshmallow root, and camomile can also aid digestion.

Tulsi Tea

Known as holy basil, tulsi is a principle herb of Ayurvedic medicine in India.

- This aromatic herb is particularly high in phytochemical antioxidants. These phytochemicals possess protective, adaptogenic, and immune-enhancing properties that can fight stress, reduce anxiety, and help promote overall health.

Green Tea

Available as loose leaf, tea bags, or as green tea matcha powder—the ground up whole leaf. Studies suggest that drinking three cups a day is enough to experience its health benefits.

- Green tea contains the amino acid L-theanine, which can work synergistically with caffeine to give the brain a boost.
- Containing less caffeine than coffee, green tea still has enough to give the body an energy lift.
- Green tea is rich in catechins, particularly epigallocatechin gallate (EGCG), an antioxidant with anticancer benefits.

Yerba Mate

Yerba mate tea is prepared by steeping the dried leaves and twigs of the mate plant in hot (not boiling) water. It has a herbal taste and is similar to green tea.

- Yerba mate is packed with antioxidants, vitamins, including B vitamins and vitamin C, and minerals such as manganese, potassium, and zinc.
- Yerba mate contains mateine, a type of caffeine, and theobromine, making it an energizing, stimulating drink. It is traditionally drunk as an aid to digestion and its stimulant qualities help you to feel full for longer.
- Studies suggest that yerba mate may help improve insulin sensitivity.

Rooibos Tea

Rooibos tea is grown from a South African bush. It is caffeine free and particularly high in antioxidants.

- Known for its anti-inflammatory and anticancer properties, rooibos is delicious either hot or cold.
- Rooibos tea contains less tannins than black tea so will not affect absorption of minerals and helps to treat insomnia.

Juices

Juicing is a good way of increasing your daily intake of fresh vegetables, fruit, and water. Juices retain all the beneficial nutrients found in the original vegetables and fruit, and these nutrients can help improve your overall health, protect against cardiovascular disease, and increase energy levels.

Nutrition: Juices are packed with health-promoting nutrients including vitamins, minerals, and phytonutrients. **Benefits:** They boost your immune system, aid digestion, and can help you to lose weight.

Green Juice

Green juices are an important drink in a raw food diet. A green juice is simply made from green vegetables, particularly leafy greens and herbs. They are composed of 80 to 90 percent vegetables with ten to 20 percent low sugar fruits, such as lemons and green apples.

- Rich in plenty of vitamins, minerals, and phytonutrients, they are easily digested.

Carrot Juice

Carrot juice and blends are another popular raw food drink. A serving of carrot juice (1 cup) has around 80 calories.

- Carrot juice is a good source of beta-carotene, potassium, vitamin C, and B vitamins, making it a particularly energizing drink.
- Carrot juice is good for keeping the skin, eyes, and immune system healthy.

Why Drink Green Smoothies?

A green smoothie is a blended drink made from leafy green vegetables and some fruit, then blended with a liquid, such as water, nut milks, herbal teas, or fermented drinks like kefir and kombucha. As they are blended these drinks are high in fiber making them good for digestive health and stabilizing blood sugar levels. Green juices can be helpful for losing weight and make an ideal pre- or postexercise drink. To keep the sugar content low, focus primarily on the greens and liquid and only use a small amount of fruit. If the drink is too bitter add a little stevia or xylitol.

If you are new to green smoothies start with milder greens, such as romaine lettuce, or spinach with celery and cucumber. Stronger tasting greens can then be used such as kale, Swiss chard, collards, parsley, and cilantro. You can further boost the nutritional content of the smoothie by adding superfood powders, nuts, seeds, superberries, and healthy fats.

Beet Juice

Beet juice is naturally sweet tasting.

- Drinking beet juice may help to lower blood pressure due to the nitrates present in beets. These are converted into nitric oxide, which helps to relax the blood vessels, improving blood flow, and lowering blood pressure.
- Beet juice can boost exercise performance and stamina.

Nondairy Milks

Nondairy milks, such as almond, cashew, hemp seed, and pumpkin seed, can be used in a wide range of raw dishes as well as drinks. You can use any nut or seed for homemade milk—simply soak the nuts or seeds overnight before draining and blending. Store-bought nut milks are available but are unlikely to be raw.

Nutrition: Nondairy milks are packed with vitamins, minerals, fiber, healthy fats, and easily digested protein.
Benefits: They are good for the immune system, help to keep the skin healthy, and strengthen bones.

Nut Milk

Nut milks are simple to make and incredibly healthy. They provide plenty of fiber, healthy fats, and protein to keep blood sugar levels balanced.

- Almond nut milk is popular as it is rich in magnesium, vitamin E, B vitamins, and protein to maintain energy levels, keep skin healthy, strengthen muscles, and strengthen bones.

Seed Milk

Seed milks often have a higher omega-3 content than nut milks. Soak the seed overnight before making into milk.

- Hemp milk is rich and creamy and a good source of easily digested protein.
- Hemp seed milk contains potassium, B vitamins, vitamins A and E, and iron.
- Pumpkin seed milk is packed with healthy fats, iron, and zinc plus calcium.

Chocolate Almond Nut Milk

GOOD FATS

This delicious creamy shake is sweetened with dates. Nut milk is very simple to make and will keep in the refrigerator for one or two days. Soak the nuts before blending to improve their digestibility, and for a creamier shake use slightly less water.

Prep: 15 mins/Soak: 8 to 12 hrs

Ingredients (around 5 servings)

1 cup (125 g) almonds, soaked in water for
    8 to 12 hours then drained
4 to 5 cups (1 to 1.2 liters) water
3 pitted dates
2 tablespoons raw cacao powder
Pinch of sea salt

Method

1 Place all the ingredients in a high speed blender and process until smooth and creamy. Strain the mixture through a strainer or nut milk bag and chill in the refrigerator until required.

PROMOTES A HEALTHY GLOWING SKIN	
Calories (per serving)	183
Protein	6.4 g
Total fat	15.5 g
of which saturated fat	1.4 g
Carbohydrates	6.9 g
of which sugars	2.6 g
Vitamins/minerals	E, B, magnesium

Fermented Drinks

Cultured or fermented drinks are very refreshing and supply the body with a range of beneficial bacteria to aid digestion and boost the immune system. Kefir and kombucha are made using a living culture that ferments and brews the drink. Others like rejuvelac are made by fermenting grains without adding a living culture.

Nutrition: Fermented drinks are packed with probiotics, amino acids, enzymes, vitamins, and minerals.
Benefits: They help with digestion, digestive problems, and metabolism, and support the immune system.

Coconut Kefir

An ancient, cultured food, kefir is rich in amino acids, enzymes, calcium, magnesium, phosphorus, and B vitamins.
- Kefir contains several major strains of friendly bacteria (*Lactobacillus caucasus*, *Leuconostoc*, *Acetobacter* species, and *Streptococcus* species) and beneficial yeasts, which aid digestion. Nut milk can be used instead of cow's milk.

Water Kefir

Water kefir is a fizzy drink made using water kefir grains, which are fermented in a sugary water solution. Kefir grains can be bought in health stores or online. You only need to buy the grains once as they will feed on the sugars and multiply.
- Water kefir can make a healthy alternative to soda and fizzy water, or can be drunk on its own.

Water Kefir

ENERGIZING

You can make water kefir at home using kefir water grains. It takes between 24 and 30 hours to ferment the cultures. Once fermented, store the kefir in the refrigerator. The longer you leave it the more sour it will become. You can also use drinking water but boil it first then let it cool before using.

Prep: 10 mins/Ferment: 24 to 48 hrs

Ingredients

2 cups (500 ml) filtered water
⅓ cup (60 g) coconut or superfine sugar
1 lemon, sliced
1 sachet (2 tablespoons) water kefir grains

Method

1 Pour the water into a clean, sterilized jar (see page 154) and stir in the sugar to dissolve. Add the lemon slices and kefir grains. Place the jar in a warm place away from bright light for 24 to 48 hours for the kefir to ferment.

2 When the kefir smells fruity and yeasty and bubbles appear on the top, strain it through a plastic strainer (don't use metal as it will harm the kefir grains). If you leave it for another day it will become fizzier.

3 Use the grains to make another batch immediately. Store in the refrigerator and drink within two weeks.

GREAT SOURCE OF PROBIOTICS	
Calories (per cup)	10
Protein	0 g
Total fat	0 g
of which saturated fat	0 g
Carbohydrates	2.0 g
of which sugars	2.0 g
Vitamins/minerals	B, K, folic acid

Kombucha

Kombucha tea, sometimes called
mushroom tea although it's not a
mushroom, is made from sweetened green
tea that's been fermented by a symbiotic
colony of bacteria and yeast (called SCOBY).
Buy kombucha SCOBY online to make your
own or purchase ready-made kombucha
from health food stores.

- Kombucha aids digestion and as it is
  a probiotic it is useful for fighting an
  overgrowth of yeast in the body.
- Kombucha helps with mental clarity
  and mood.
- This tea contains glucosamines, which
  are beneficial for cartilage structure and
  to prevent arthritis.

Rejuvelac

Rejuvelac is made using cereal grains, such
as rye, barley, oats, wheat, or buckwheat,
that are soaked then sprouted for three
days before fermenting for another two to
three days. Store in the refrigerator.

- Rejuvelac contains friendly bacteria to
  support a healthy digestive system.
- This is an excellent source of B vitamins
  and vitamins C and E.

Why Might You Avoid Alcohol?

While wine is considered a raw food (beer and distilled liquors are not) it is important to remember that alcohol can upset blood sugar balance, burden the liver with toxins, and irritate the gut. If you are choosing alcohol it is a good idea to select organic wine that is low in sulfites or without added sulfites. Many people who follow a raw food diet do so to improve detoxification and cleansing, so for this reason you may wish to avoid alcohol altogether or limit your intake. Some people following a raw diet tend to feel the effects of alcohol more strongly. This may be because your body becomes more efficient at absorption so the alcohol hits you more quickly. If you do want to drink alcohol then eat plenty of alkaline foods before and after drinking to alleviate some of the acidity in the stomach.

Raw Food Dos and Don'ts

What to Include

- Fresh fruits and vegetables, frozen fruit and vegetables
- Ready sprouted seeds and beans or dried beans/seeds to sprout
- Nuts and seeds: includes raw nuts and seeds (whole and ground), activated nuts, seed and nut oils, nut and seed butters and spreads, tahini, buckwheat groats, quinoa, coconut flakes, dry unsweetened coconut
- Oils: coconut oil, omega blended oils, flaxseed, chia, and hemp oils, extra virgin olive oil, avocado oil, walnut oil
- Sea vegetables
- Condiments: sea salt, herbal salts, garlic salt, freshly ground black pepper, nutritional yeast flakes, vanilla extract,

spices and herbs, apple cider vinegar, rice, balsamic, and red wine vinegars, Nama shoyu (raw soy sauce), tamari, white miso paste, marinated sundried tomatoes, mustard, olives
- Sweeteners: xylitol, raw honey, bee and flower pollen, coconut sugar, yacon syrup, stevia, lucuma, dried fruits
- Raw fermented foods: sauerkraut, raw pickles, coconut yogurt, water kefir, raw milk kefir and coconut kefir, kombucha, rejuvelac
- Superfoods: algae superfoods, chlorella, Klamath lake blue green algae, spirulina, bee products
- Superberry powders: acai, amla, goji, inca, baobab, camu camu, macqui berry, lucuma, mulberry
- Raw chocolate: cacao powder, butter, raw chocolates, cacao beans, and nibs
- Superfood roots, grasses, leaves, and vegetables: maca, moringa leaf, barley grass, wheatgrass, supergreen blends, schizandra, ginseng, he shou wu, shilajit, green tea, and matcha tea powder
- Medicinal mushrooms: chaga, cordyceps, maitake, reishi (fresh, dried, powdered blends, and tinctures)
- Raw meat, dairy, eggs, and fish (optional, not vegan).

What to Avoid

- Processed foods, ready meals
- Any foods heated above 118°F (48°C)
- Candies and artificial sweeteners
- Sodas, squash, etc.
- Cooked grains, beans, and pulses
- Baked goods: breads, pasta, cookies, crackers, etc.
- Pasteurized dairy products
- Roasted nuts and seeds
- Soy foods (miso may be included)
- Wheat (except wheatgrass), breads, pastries, pastas, etc.
- Refined sugars and syrups
- Table salt.

Glossary

Amino acids—these are the building blocks of muscle-building protein. They carry out important functions, have a key role in the storage of nutrients, and help in wound healing.

Antioxidants—these protect our bodies against the damaging effects of free radicals. Vitamins C, E, beta-carotene, and selenium are antioxidants.

Beta-carotene—a pigment found in large quantities in orange-fleshed and dark green fruit and vegetables and is turned into vitamin A by the body.

Coconut aminos—made from coconut sap and sea salt, it has a salty taste similar to soy sauce.

Detoxification—the biochemical process that transforms non-water soluble toxins and metabolites into water soluble compounds that can be excreted in urine, sweat, bile, or feces.

Fats—compounds of carbon, hydrogen, and oxygen atoms that exist in chains of varying lengths, shapes, and orders. They are one of the vital nutrients required by the body for both sustaining energy and the construction and maintenance of "structural" elements, such as cell membranes.

Free radical—a highly chemically reactive molecule often containing oxygen that can cause damage to cells in the body.

Glycemic index (GI)—rates ingredients and dishes according to the rate at which a carbohydrate food breaks down into sugars and enters the bloodstream.

Inulin—a starchy substance found in a wide variety of fruits, vegetables, and herbs, including wheat, onions, bananas, leeks, artichokes, and asparagus. Inulin is not digested or absorbed in the stomach. It supports the growth of a friendly bacteria that are associated with

improving the health of the bowels as well as general health.

Monounsaturated fat—these fatty acids contain just one double bond in their fatty acid chain. The more double bonds a fatty acid boasts, the more "fluid" it is. They are generally liquid at room temperature.

Nutritional yeast—a yeast supplement available as flakes rich in B vitamins. Its taste varies from nutty to cheesy. Used to enhance nutrients and flavors in dishes and for making nut cheeses.

Oxidative stress—this arises when there is an imbalance between the damage caused by free radicals and the body's ability to protect from these chemicals.

Phytonutrients—compounds found in plants, nuts, seeds, whole grains, and beans that help prevent various diseases.

Polyunsaturated fats—these fats have more than one double bond in their fatty acid chain. They tend to be liquid even when refrigerated. They include omega-3 and -6 fatty acids.

Prebiotics—nondigestible food ingredients (e.g. inulin, certain fibers) that promote the growth of beneficial microorganisms in the intestines.

Probiotic—beneficial microorganisms that live in the body primarily in the gastrointestinal tract.

Raw vegan diet—this diet excludes all food of animal origin, and all food cooked above 118°F (48°C). It includes raw vegetables and fruits, nuts and nut pastes, grain and legume sprouts, seeds, plant oils, sea vegetables, herbs, and fresh juices.

Saturated fats—saturated fats have all available carbon bonds paired with hydrogen atoms. They are solid at room temperature.

Vegan—a person who adheres to a strict vegetarian or pure plant-based diet. A vegan consumes no animal products at all but may eat cooked vegan foods unlike a raw vegan.

Index

Credits

Picture credits
(t)= top, (c)= center, (b)= bottom, (l)= left, (r)= right

Shutterstock.com: 7 Olha Afanasieva; 8-9 Jill Chen; 11 Jill Chen; 12 wavebreakmedia; 13 Kzenon; 15 sarsmis; 17 Minerva Studio; 18 Dream79; 19 Drozdowski; 20 hutch photography; 21 bonchan; 22(l) elena moiseeva; 22(r) catalin eremia; 23 Karl Allgaeuer; 25 Boumen Japet; 26 Sergey Dubrov; 27 Brent Hofacker; 28 iva; 30 Gayvoronskaya_Yana; 31 Maridav; 34 Monkey Business Images; 35 Jiri Hera; 36 seiseis; 37(t) wavebreakmedia; 37(b) bitt24; 38-39 yonibunga; 40 Brent Hofacker; 42(c) Lightspring; 42(b) Brent Hofacker; 43(t) B. and E. Dudzinscy; 43(c) AnjelikaGr; 43(b) GreenArt Photography; 44(t) Andrii Opanasenko; 44(c) Kunertus; 44(b) peuceta; 45(t) Nadalina; 45(c) Brent Hofacker; 45(b) tab62; 47 Foodio; 48(t) teleginatania; 48(c) Alena Haurylik; 48(b) Brent Hofacker; 49 stockcreations; 50(t) Dusan Zidar; 50(b) Gayvoronskaya_Yana; 51(t) Olha Afanasieva; 51(c) Brent Hofacker; 51(b) Zigzag Mountain Art; 52(t) Zoeytoja; 52(c) paulista; 52(b) Yulia von Eisenstein; 53 Simone Voigt; 54(c) bitt24; 54(b) Valentyn Volkov; 55(t) Kati Molin; 55(c) Africa Studio; 55(b) Orlio; 56(t) Dream79; 56(b) Dream79; 57 alisafarov; 58(c) Gayvoronskaya_Yana; 58(b) sarsmis; 59(t) Melpomene; 59(c) Le Do; 59(b) Razmarinka; 60 Phrompas; 61(t) Quanthem; 61(c) Sea Wave; 61(b) TRL; 63 neil langan; 64(t) Es75; 64(c) Phrompas; 64(b) Space Monkey Pics; 65(c) Lukas Gojda; 65(b) mama_mia; 66(t) Dream79; 66(c) Yulia von Eisenstein; 66(b) GaynorJ; 67 Brent Hofacker; 68(t) Cary Bates; 68(c) pilipphoto; 68(b) pilipphoto; 69 Lilyana Vynogradova; 70(c) Gayvoronskaya_Yana; 70(b) Ekaterina Kondratova; 71(t) roroto12p; 71(c) Aprilphoto; 71(b) mama_mia; 73 sarsmis; 75(t) Only Fabrizio; 75(c) Andrey Starostin; 75(b) Reika; 76(t) yasuhiro amano; 76(c) Destinyweddingstudio; 76(b) Africa Studio; 77(t) JKB Stock; 77(c) marekuliasz; 79 Jan Mika; 80 Lukas Gojda; 82(c) marekuliasz; 82(b) joannawnuk; 83(t) wasanajai; 83(b) Brent Hofacker; 84 smuay; 85(t) Boumen Japet; 85(c) joannawnuk; 85(b) Chamille White; 87 Kati Molin; 88(c) Elena Schweitzer; 88(b) Andreja Donko; 89(t) inacio pires; 89(c) ailenn; 89(b) Alexander Mazurkevich; 90 Tim UR; 91 Liv friis-larsen; 92(t) Dionisvera; 92(c) Olha Afanasieva; 93(t) minicase; 93(b) vainillaychile; 94(t) leungchopan; 94(c) ThamKC; 94(b) wasanajai; 95(t) wasanajai; 95(b) Sommai; 96 Brent Hofacker; 98(t) Brandon Bourdages; 98(c) Drozdowski; 98(b) Mariusz S. Jurgielewicz; 99(t) tinglee1631; 99(c) Nikitin Victor; 99(b) Li Chaoshu; 100(t) KPG_Payless; 100(c) Creatista; 100(b) dabjola; 101 marco mayer; 102 suraj p singh; 104(c) Ariene Studio; 104(b) Elena Elisseeva; 105(t) HandmadePictures; 105(c) Toni Genes; 105(b) Jiang Hongyan; 106(t) Jiri Hera; 106(c) Olga_Phoenix; 106(b) bzanchi; 107 Olga Miltsova; 108 leonori; 110(c) Africa Studio; 110(b) Goncharuk Maksim; 111(t) MaraZe; 111(c) Volosina; 111(b) Marina Onokhina; 113 Anna_Pustynnikova; 114(c) Sea Wave; 114(b) Jag_cz; 115(t) Anna Hoychuk; 115(c) Lukas Gojda; 115(b) Africa Studio; 116 Maks Narodenko; 117 Douglas Freer; 118(C) Coffee Lover; 118(b) inacio pires; 119(t) Karen Sarraga; 119(c) Phonlawat_778; 119(b) Valentyn Volkov; 121 vanillaechoes; 122(t) Obstinada; 122(c) Li Chaoshu; 122(b) gabczi; 123(t) NorGal; 123(c) al1962; 123(b) Karissaa; 124(t) Pattakorn Uttarasak; 124(c) inacio pires; 124(b) Lesya Dolyuk; 125(t) OZMedia; 125(c) Elena

Shashkina; 125(b) Sea Wave; 127 MShev; 128(c) Wiktory; 128(b) annata78; 129(t) sarsmis; 129(c) Zadorozhna Natalia; 129(b) Sea Wave; 130(t) Lukas Gojda; 130(c) ziashusha; 130(b) Subbotina Anna; 131 Phonlawat_778; 132(c) marekuliasz; 132(b) id-art; 133(t) GreenTree; 133(c) papillondream; 133(b) guentermanaus; 134(t) HandmadePictures; 134(c) gresei; 134(b) Ildi Papp; 135(t) marekuliasz; 135(c) nookieme; 135(b) Photoraidz; 136 draconus; 137 tanjichica; 138 Brent Hofacker; 140(c) successo images; 140(b) grafvision; 141(t) Gayvoronskaya_Yana; 141(c) Sea Wave; 141(b) Amawasri Pakdara; 142(t) Shawn Hempel; 142(b) Dionisvera; 143(c) Simone van den Berg; 143(b) Jiri Hera; 144(t) marekuliasz; 144(c) Sea Wave; 144(b) HandmadePictures; 145(t) Gayvoronskaya_Yana; 145(c) CJansuebsri; 145(b) Bruno D'Andrea; 146 Andrii Gorulko; 147 Melle V; 149 A. Aleksandravicius; 150 successo images; 152(c) BGSmith; 152(b) Gayvoronskaya_Yana; 153(t) Foodio; 153(c) Gayvoronskaya_Yana; 153(b) mama_mia; 154 gresei; 155 Sea Wave; 156(t) blackboard1965; 156(c) Foodpictures; 156(b) Liv friis-larsen; 157 o_lesyk; 159 GreenArt Photography; 160 Africa Studio; 162(t) Gayvoronskaya_Yana; 162(c) Africa Studio; 162(b) Dusan Zidar; 163(t) HandmadePictures; 163(c) jurgajurga; 163(b) mama_mia; 164(t) picturepartners; 164(c) Sea Wave; 164(b) mama_mia; 165 Lorraine Kourafas; 166 Evgeny Karandaev; 167 Pachanon; 169 Africa Studio; 171 Anna_Pustynnikova; 172 Evgeny Karandaev; 174(c) Olyina; 174(b) MaraZe; 175(t) deeepblue; 175(c) deeepblue; 175(b) Post424; 176(t) Tish1; 176(c) matka_Wariatka; 176(b) Jiri Hera; 177 Maxim Khytra; 178(c) grafvision; 178(b) bitt24; 179(t) Anch; 179(c) ravipat; 179(b) marekuliasz; 180(t) Aliwak; 180(c) kttpngart; 180(b) Cindy Creighton; 181 Africa Studio; 182 deniss09; 183 GeNik; 185 phoelix; 186 zstock; 188(c) joannawnuk; 188(b) Henk Jacobs; 189(c) grintan; 189(b) Wichy; 190(t) Olga Miltsova; 190(b) deeepblue; 191(t) Ferumov; 191(b) MSPhotographic; 192(c) Maxim Khytra; 192(b) bitt24; 193(t) Teri Virbickis; 193(b) Dream79; 194(c) Sea Wave; 194(b) mama_mia; 195 Edita Piu; 196(c) minadezhda; 196(b) blackboard1965; 197 blackboard1965; 198(t) GreenArt Photography; 198(b) tacar; 199 Opolja; 200 Stephanie Frey; 202 Olga Pink; 203 Lena Gabrilovich.

Female outline: 81, 103, 139, 151, 161, 187 Anna Rassadnikova.

Male outline: 41, 97, 109, 173 Turovsky.

Creative Commons: 77(b) EugeneZelenko; 92(b) JMK; 95(c) Chirag Jindal.

While every effort has been made to credit contributors, Quantum would like to apologize should there have been any omissions or errors.

Christine Bailey
www.christinebailey.co.uk

Christine is a member of the British Association for Applied Nutrition and Nutritional Therapy (BANT), Complementary and Natural Healthcare Council (CNHC), and the NHS Directory of Complementary Therapists. Christine adheres to the strict BANT Code of Ethics and Practice.